THE INDIFFERENCE OF BIRDS

DAILY REFLECTIONS ON

THE PHILOSOPHY OF ZHUANGZI

SCOTT P. BRADLEY

Published by BookLocker.com, Inc., St. Petersburg, Florida.

Printed on acid-free paper.

BookLocker.com, Inc.

2016

First Edition

CONTENTS

INTRODUCTION

This is an assemblage of posts which have appeared on my website over the course of about one year. As posts they take brevity as a virtue—something one can easily read while sipping the morning's coffee before heading to work. There is no reason why this introduction should not follow suit.

The topic is the philosophy of Zhuangzi (Chuang-Tzu), a Fourth Century B.C. Chinese philosopher of vaguely "Daoist" persuasion. This is found in the first seven chapters, called the Inner Chapters, of the book that bears his name. This, at least, I assume as a matter of convenience. Scholars debate whether he was in fact the author or whether these chapters are the work of several hands. For my purposes, this matters little. I am not a follower of a presumed "sage" or of a sacred text, but the creator of my own dao who finds that these writings speak to life as I experience it.

At my reading, the message of the Inner Chapters is in many ways unique and I do not, therefore, interpret them in the context of the remaining chapters of the *Zhuangzi* or other classical "Daoist" texts such as the *Laozi*, although they sometimes provide a supporting voice. I let them speak for themselves.

Brevity also has the advantage of suggestiveness. Rather than being spoon-fed, one is invited to think. No post or series of posts can do justice to the topic at hand, in any case. Moreover, the post topics have no special sequential order, and thus may sometimes reference posts or themes still to come. It is hoped, however, that a more or less singular and coherent vision will emerge when all the posts have been read.

As for this vision, it is entirely my own. I make no claim to having accurately interpreted Zhuangzi. Nor do I wish to suggest that my vision should be adopted by others. This, I believe, is just as Zhuangzi would have it. "Daos are made by walking them", he wrote, and there are as many daos as there are pairs of feet to walk them.

All quotes from the *Zhuangzi* are from Brook Ziporyn's *Zhuangzi: The Essential Writings, with Selections from Traditional Commentaries* which I believe faithfully captures much of the elusive spirit of Zhuangzi. Since he has numbered passages and important lines in the Inner Chapters so as to index them to the appended commentaries, this makes for easy referencing of the quotes. A simplified (2:15) for example will thus refer to Ziporyn's translation. Those passages not so numbered will be designated by a chapter number and page number, (23; p 97). I have taken the liberty to revert to the transliterations Dao and de, rather than to retain his "Course" and "virtue", which though are applicable in some cases, do not always seem so.

The aforementioned website is at www.engagingwithzhuangzi.com. Contact can be made there.

SERIAL REFLECTIONS

A NEW PHILOSOPHICAL DAOISM

DAOISM

I – XIII

I

I have come to the conclusion that the best way to present my take away from Zhuangzi is to admit that it cannot claim to represent even an approximately definitive interpretation of his intended meanings. These must forever remain matters for informed guesses. And this, again at my reading, was precisely the purpose of his intended ambiguity. There are several reasons why such a strategy is necessary and effective from the point of view of Daoist sensibilities.

There are parallels here with Socrates' maieutic method (his tutorial midwifery) and Kierkegaard's "indirect communication" (his adoption of various pseudonyms for the purpose of presenting different perspectives on one idea). The point is to make us engage in a kind of critical thinking that is itself a kind of existential engagement. It's as much about doing and being as it is about knowing. The knowing arises from the being and the doing.

Among Zhuangzi's descriptive representations of the attributes of sagacity is the wonderful suggestion that we "release the mind to play among all expressions (*de*)". Where there are set beliefs and formulae there can be no such play. An absolutist position on the nature of Zhuangzi's Daoism would be as antithetical to this freedom as any other. We must hold our position lightly. We must forget the fish trap, the words, in our having obtained the fish, our freedom, lest we lose it once again.

Though Zhuangzi critiques the sectarian positions of the Confucians and Mohists, and replaces theirs with a more inclusive one of his own, we understand that he understood that sense in which his and theirs were the same. His was "better" by virtue of its inclusiveness—the formation of a sense of oneness being his understanding of Dao—but it could only be so when it self-effaced in an appreciation of the sameness, the equanimity and oneness, of all *de*.

In this context, we can critique the positions that others take vis-à-vis the nature of Zhuangzi's Daoism without that becoming sectarian. I feel strongly that many, if not most, very knowledgeable scholars miss the spirit of Zhuangzi's philosophy entirely. The presumption of such an opinion does not escape me. Nor am I unaware of the dangers of sectarianism in this regard. It is these concerns that have inspired this series.

II

Zhuangzi's intended ambiguity means that any interpretation of him must necessarily involve a personal engagement that can only lead to a unique perspective. This, of course, is precisely what he wanted us to understand through his argument for perspectival relativism. Our cognitive responses to the world arise from our position within it. In this blog I attempt to share my own take on Zhuangzi's philosophical Daoism, and this can only be a new philosophical Daoism. It cannot be "the" new philosophical Daoism, but can nonetheless contribute to the evolution of other points of view just as it is itself so evolving.

Zhuangzi invites us to understand how our perspectives are all different and unique. He also suggests we realize how they are the same. All things can be "seen from the point of view of their sameness". How are my views on Zhuangzi the same as every other? They are all both right and wrong. They are all right from the perspective of the individual, and wrong from the perspective of some other. But as one scholar has pointed out, this trajectory toward sameness leads Zhuangzi to imply more emphatically that they are all wrong. They are all wrong to the extent that they think they are right—and that they think they are right is at the most immediate level unavoidable. This broadening perspective helps us to "release the mind to play among the harmony of all *de* [expressions]". Their harmony is their sameness in all being wrong (as well as right).

Knowing we are unavoidably wrong enables us to make the best use of whatever "fish trap" we fabricate while simultaneously "forgetting" it. To be "empty" is not to contain nothing, but to contain everything in unfixed and ungrasping openness. Liu Xianxin

(1896-1932) sees this as defining the difference between Buddhist and Daoist sensibilities: "The main principle of Buddhism is Emptiness: nothing is wanted; all is to be abandoned. The main principle of Daoism is vastness: everything is wanted; all is to be included" (Ziporyn, p 137).

How are they the same? From the Zhuangzian point of view, they are both simply upayic strategies, the values of which can only be determined by their effectiveness as judged by their respective adherents. They are both wrong to the extent that they think that they alone are right. And they are both wrong to the extent that they think they represent the truth of things.

Both have their benefits; both deliver some goods. Fortunately, you don't have to get it "right" to get it—whatever "it" may be.

III

You don't have to get it right to get it.

This series is inspired by my current reading of Harold Roth's *Original Tao: Inward Training (*Nei-yeh*) and the Foundations of Taoist Mysticism.* I have long been pushing back against the near ubiquitous tendency to conflate Zhuangzi's philosophy with that of more religious forms of Daoism that preceded and followed it. Roth's project is to do precisely this. "Daoism", its many diverse expressions notwithstanding, is woven into a single cloth. Breathing meditation, the "attainment of the Dao", the inner accumulation of something called *qi (ch'i)*—all of them essentially religious practices and conceptions—are taken to be the foundation for all classical Daoist mystical philosophies. This is equivalent to equating the three "great" monotheistic religions, Judaism, Christianity and Islam, because they all speak of "God".

My understanding of Zhuangzi leads me to believe that he consciously wished to offer an alternative kind of mysticism, one free of all metaphysical hocus-pocus and definitive technique. When he suggested we depend on nothing, he meant it.

Thus, if there is something to "get"—an experience of freedom, oneness and tranquility—then it does not require any particular knowledge or method. It is something that is inherently possible for human beings to experience quite apart from any imagined extra-mundane "realities". And the means to that experience are many. There is no "right way". You don't have to get it right to get it.

Why Zhuangzi chose this way of non-dependence I do not know. I do know that it speaks to my own need for a post-religious means of coping with the unavoidable existential dangle of the human experience.

Yes, it is all just coping. That's the point. It's not about realizing the Truth. It's not about being saved. It's not about realizing our "true" self or purpose. It's about being human.

This philosophical Daoism is likely not Zhuangzi's philosophical Daoism, though it is an attempt to be approximatingly so. It doesn't matter.

IV

Zhuangzi is clearly taking us for a ride. He's having us on. Missing this is missing the spirit of his philosophy. Consider his use of Confucius. Sometimes he is the protagonist advocating for something suggestive of Zhuangzi's philosophy; other times he's the arch-Confucian, the voice of an imposed morality. There is method in this madness. There is a message in this medium. And part of that message is that we should not take any of it too seriously. Seriousness and literalism are the antithesis of the spirit of Zhuangzi, the spirit of play.

When we play, we take things both very seriously and unseriously at once. We agree to follow arbitrary rules and to give our all to win. We agree to pretend that it matters whether we win or lose. But we know that winning and losing are of no ultimate value at all. It's how we play the game that counts. This is called good sportsmanship. The Zhuangzian sage is a good sportsperson; she takes life very seriously even while knowing it isn't serious at all. And sages are extremely rare.

When Zhuangzi has a few of his made-up characters discuss the likely facticity of a fantastic sage who subsists on only wind and dew, and who rides on the backs of dragons, what is he up to? In agreement with the madman who proposed such a sage and his belief in him, the interlocutor who is the most sagacious seems to suggest that this is entirely possible. Are we also meant to believe? Or are we meant to simply open our minds to the possibility of experiences beyond the usual?

These are Zhuangzi's "big words"—"useless" from the point of view of "winning" the game of life. But if winning is the all-in-all, then life becomes so serious an affair that it is no fun at all. It is the useless understanding that life need not be taken so seriously that becomes the most useful thing of all.

When Zhuangzi speaks of *qi*, the supposed stuff of which all things are composed and, for some the most rarified form of which the sage accumulates so as to become "spiritual", is he telling us he believes in any such thing or project? Or is he simply making use of the materials at hand to make another point altogether?

When we take Zhuangzi literally we make of him yet another overly serious advocate for fixed religious beliefs and projects. We destroy his message and rob him of the spirit of play.

V

If we take all within the Inner Chapters of the *Zhuangzi* as the work of Zhuangzi, there is considerable internal evidence that he was aware of the beliefs and practices of, if not the *Nei Yeh* ("Inner Training") chapter of the anthology called the *Kuanzi*, than at least the school of thought of which it is representative. Some of "Confucius's" instructions to his disciple Yan in Chapter Four could be taken as clear allusions to this likely contemporaneous work. (Some have apparently questioned the authenticity of this passage, though I have only read Liu Xiaogan's (*Classifying the Zhuangzi Chapters*) dismissal of these doubts.) Zhuangzi makes use of these as he does other materials at hand. But, as a scholar (whose identity I do not have permission to share) has recently pointed out, he also speaks of Confucian virtues without being a Confucian, uselessness without being a Mohist, and "white horses" without being a Logician. If Zhuangzi "released [his] mind to play in the harmony of all *de*", then he could make use of any of them without our having to believe he fixedly attached to any particular one.

Zhuangzi may very well have practiced some form of breathing meditation; only I would contend that this would not have included the metaphysical beliefs of his contemporaries who also did so. The difference is between religious-mindedness and utterly unfixed openness. This distinction is important because, at my reading, Zhuangzi's entire vision turns on making use of our (useless) utter not-knowing. The practice of non-dependence, which I take to be an overarching attribute of his proposed dao, includes not relying on any beliefs about the nature of reality. We do not become "empty" in order to be filled by a "something", but because empty is what we are and what we must remain if we wish to live authentically.

Admittedly, Zhuangzi is largely what we make him to be. This is how I make him to be because this is what I need him to be if he is to be of use to me, someone who cannot do the religious thing. However, in having taken him as I have, I can now make use of him as I believe he made use of others. In this sense, the "truth" of Zhuangzi's philosophy does not matter. This is what I mean by "a new philosophical Daoism"; one that makes use of the materials at hand so as to evolve a uniquely personal strategy for the enjoyment of life.

Thanks for the leg up, Zhuangzi—I can take it from here.

VI

This series is also largely inspired by my need to make periodic disclaimers. For all my often apparently unequivocal pronouncements regarding the character of Zhuangzi's Daoism, I wish to make clear that I do not believe I or anyone else can be sure of what we speak. This, I believe, is precisely how Zhuangzi would have had it. (Here I go again.) This is his whole point. Depend on nothing. Release into not-knowing. Live life as it manifests in you, not as you might otherwise wish it to be. Add nothing to the process of life. Don't flee from the actual experience of being human, but rather make creative use of it. Let your inherent adriftedness be an occasion for your wandering, rather than for clinging to chimeric moorings.

Do this. Or don't. It doesn't matter all that much. All is well in any case. Isn't it? It is or it isn't. But from the cosmic perspective it is whether it is or it is not. Isn't it?

Every presentation of Daoism, at least of the philosophic variety, is a new philosophical Daoism. There is no such thing as a fixed definition and experience of Daoism. Why would we wish it to be otherwise? Why would we wish to follow rather than to lead? Because, unless we are self-deceived, we know we can only lead ourselves, and that is a lonely experience. Why would we wish to believe in the already-fixed rather than to create anew? Because, unless we are delusional, we know that whatever we create is as ridiculously tenuous as we know ourselves to be. It's so much easier and more comforting to abrogate responsibility to external authorities which somehow escape the scrutiny of doubt.

Then there is the problem of personal reality. I realize little of my own blabber. But surely the blabbering sages realized their own blabber. That's why they're sages, right? We can believe that what we believe is real, because we believe that it was real for someone else. This is called begging the question, placing the conclusion in the premise. Sages exist because they say they do—or more sagaciously, someone else says they do.

"The ancients called this, 'fleeing from the Lord's dangle'." I call it fleeing from your real experience. Whether there actually are or were sages, we live more authentically when we leave the question moot.

VII

"Daos are made by walking them." Is there anyone who does not have a dao? We all walk a dao. Daos are unavoidable. Can we walk another's dao? We can try. This is what we mostly do. Only now it is an inauthentic dao. Now it is a dao that fails to express our own individual experience; and this amounts to a flight from our own self-experience.

Are there then authentic and inauthentic daos? There are. But of course there is also neither. There are only daos that more closely approximate one or the other. Perfection and purity are only ideal abstractions—only helpful when understood as such; only full when empty.

Can we be authentically inauthentic? Sure; that's called honesty. Can we be inauthentically authentic? Sure; that's called hypocrisy and self-deception. Can we be both at once? Could we be otherwise?

"Daos are made by walking them." Zhuangzi says so because he wishes to show their relative nature. We create our own unique daos. All daos are human creations. There's no true Dao (Guidance) out there that we can discover. Heaven will not guide us. Any spoken Dao is not-Dao, but just a dao. In this he agrees with Laozi. Why is it that so much "Daoism" also agrees, only to once again speak of "attaining the Dao"? This Dao, though ineffable, is a something that can guide us mysteriously, mystically. Not to worry—there is True Guidance after all.

This is not Zhuangzi's dao. In Zhuangzi's dao, Dao remains silent; it is present only as an absence. It is yin to our yang. It entices us to release into Mystery. Mystery does not yang. It does not guide. It provides no answers.

Because Dao provides no one dao, no single dao alone reflects Dao. All daos are human creations; and in this sense they are all equal. All daos are Dao, where Dao is this apparent Happening and the mystery of this Happening. In this they are also all equal.

For Zhuangzi, psychological Dao is the only attainable Dao, and this entails the convergence of all daos; the realization of a oneness. This is the equalization of all daos, and the "attainment of Dao".

All daos, whether authentic or inauthentic, are equal and affirmable. But they do not all equally contribute to human flourishing. We can therefore also judge between them. But can we judge for others? How much authenticity can any particular person take? How much inauthenticity is unavoidable and even necessary? We can only find out for ourselves by consciously walking our own daos.

VIII

The declaration that I am doing a new philosophical Daoism sounds pretentious to say the least. But I say so only because I am unable to discover an old one. Several are there to be sure, but I cannot be sure what they are. Nor do I believe that anyone else can, however more scholarly. Indeed, scholarship might easily be an impediment. Scholarship easily misses the forest for the trees; and scholarship often fears the subjective commitment that alone can discover the spirit behind the words. Thus, everyone who thoughtfully engages with Daoism is creating their own new philosophical Daoism.

Whoever is reading this is likely doing so out of an interest in Daoism or some parallel philosophy. To my thinking, you too are creating your own unique philosophy of life. And that is about the best we can do. If there is no one, true solution to life's contingencies then whatever response we formulate will be our own. But we don't build from nothing; we make use of all the materials at hand. I like to make use of Zhuangzi. His sense of things speaks well to my experience. Or, at least, my experience finds that sense in him.

The proclamation of the "death of God" offends many, but I think Nietzsche wasn't so much trying to offend as to bear witness to a cultural paradigm shift. This represents a great parting of ways. Is Truth out there waiting to be discovered, or are we required to create our own? My experience leads me to choose the latter. It's a scary and daunting task, but such is life. It's also liberating. There is no Truth. That's one less thing to worry about. (This is not to say there is no Truth, but only that there is none for me.)

Everyone's building their own philosophy of life; everyone's just trying to cope. Perhaps those who can believe find it easier than others, but I'm not so sure. Perhaps those who don't question much find it easier than those that do. This seems more likely. Indeed, these, like newborn babes, may be reflections of sagacity.

Socrates' famous dictum that "the unexamined life is not worth living" is as false as it is true. If every life is not worth living, then no life is. Still, for those so disposed—those who need to question—an enquiry into what can make for a happier life is well worth the effort. And, quite frankly, it seems likely that the benefit lies mostly in the effort rather than in the results. Thinking can be fun. And it helps one get through the day.

IX

There is mysticism in Zhuangzi's suggested response to life. This mysticism does not, however, fit within the standard representations of mysticism. One of these is the belief that one can "unite" with some ultimate reality. In the case of most representations of Daoism, this would be "the Dao", the Source that interpenetrates all reality. There is also *qi* (*ch'i*), the "vital force" that gives life (and being) to all things. This can be "accumulated" by the sage, extending her life and giving her inner power. The relationship between these two is unclear.

Secondly, when one unites with this ultimate reality, one gains insight into the Truth. Since Dao interpenetrates all things, communion with Dao enables an understanding of all things. This can lead to powers of prognostication.

Thirdly, this union with metaphysical Dao and accumulation of *qi* is accomplished through the practice of breathing meditation whereby one empties one's mind of all thought and emotion.

If this is the mysticism of Daoism, then Zhuangzi was clearly not a Daoist. His mysticism takes the absence of any and all imagined metaphysical realities as its point of departure. It begins and ends in not-knowing. This is fundamental; absent this and his philosophy collapses. As for meditative practice, he may very well have done some, but its purpose and importance would have been much different. Reliance on any "technique" is depending on something, and for Zhuangzi dependence on nothing lies at the heart of his mystical movement. We need only witness the near obsession of those who do advocate such practice, to see that Zhuangzi did not share this commitment. His allusions to meditative practice, like his narratives generally, seem designed more to suggest positive outcomes than the means to their realization.

Alternatively, we could broaden our understanding of Daoism to include Zhuangzi's skeptical branch. But he does, in fact, seem to be such an anomaly within the context of Daoism that it might be best to remove him altogether. Daoists, needless to say, would find no need to do so, since they have thoroughly molded him to their purposes.

This is not about the right way versus the wrong way, or even the correct way to interpret Zhuangzi. What is important to me is to preserve the way in which I have molded him to *my* purposes. This is not to suggest that there are no textual justifications for my understanding of Zhuangzi, but only that these are prejudiced by my experience. Nor do I wish to *depend on* however I understand Zhuangzi; having caught my fish, I'd rather eat it than the fish trap.

X

Zhuangzi's mysticism is quite simple. Finding ourselves embedded in Mystery, we affirm it so completely for that to amount to releasing ourselves entirely into it. And this amounts to a sense of oneness with it. One with Process, what process could possibly harm us?

Mystery is as much "in here" as it is "out there". Absolutely everything is Mystery. The totality of our experience is Mystery. Thus, releasing into Mystery is releasing into ourselves, our most immediate experience of Mystery. It's the affirmation of our entire human experience. It's shouting "Yes!" to life.

There is much in life that we do not particularly like; suffering, death, harm done to others, and our own failings top the list. Affirming the Totality entails affirming these as well. This is what makes such a movement so difficult, especially in the case of evil. Yet, affirming these as the expression of Mystery does not mean complete acquiescence to them. This is the importance of "walking two roads at once", the ability to hold to a cosmic view and a human view simultaneously. The former informs the latter so as to insure our concerns do not destroy our peace and thankfulness. We rightfully attempt to extend life, prevent suffering, curb harm to others, and improve ourselves. Only now these are done in the light of a broader context.

On what basis can we justify affirming the Totality? Isn't this just an arbitrary determination? From the point of view of reason, it is. But from the point of view of life, it is not. This is what life is and does. Life is affirmation. It is its own celebration. With reference to the protestations of reason, Zhuangzi suggests we not "add to the process of life". Let the broader experience of life guide us, rather than the worries of the deliberating mind. Reason might call this "circular", but then so is reason's own self-justification. That's why it's all Mystery.

XI

One of the most evocative metaphors that Zhuangzi uses to suggest releasing ourselves into Mystery is "hiding the world in the world". If we hide our boat in a swamp, someone will eventually come along and steal it. There was somewhere into which the boat could be lost—somewhere out there in the broader world. But what if we were to hide our boat in the whole world? Where then could it be lost? Hiding the world in the world is hiding not only our boat, but also everything else, including our most precious selves, in the greater world (Mystery) where nothing can be lost.

Zhuangzi uses this metaphor in the context of our fear of death, the apparent loss of ourselves. If, instead of clinging to this particular identity, we release ourselves into the apparently ceaseless transformation of all identities, release into Transformation, where is there any room for us to be lost? This obviously requires loosening our grip on our self-identity. Just as we must be willing to "lose" the boat in order to never lose it, so also must we "lose" ourselves so as to have nothing to lose.

This, I think, is primarily what Zhuangzi has in mind when he entreats us to "just be empty, nothing more". To be empty is to have no-fixed-identity. It is to enjoy our present identity as part of the larger context wherein all identities are forever transforming.

Is this simply a ploy, an intellectual and palliative sleight of hand designed to ease our passing? For the most part, I think it is. It is essentially a psychological strategy for coping with the existential dangle—our ever not-knowing despite our hunger for the same—of our inherent experience. However, given our point of departure that all is Mystery, such a strategy seems both intellectually or existentially honest. We must remember that none of this is about the "truth" of things, but only always about our experience of things. Such is life.

Still, this is more than just an intellectual exercise; there is mysticism involved here; and this entails transformative experience. Nice things happen when we release into Mystery. Thankfulness happens. (And thankfulness feels good.) Tranquility happens. (Of which I can at least testify to some fleeting approximation—let's not get all absolutist and silly, not to mention dishonest.)

XII

The concept of no-fixed-identity suggests that one can release one's grip on one's particular self-identity while still enjoying the same. The spirit of play can help to illustrate this arrangement. Play requires taking the game seriously, while simultaneously understanding that it is in fact just a game, something made up for our enjoyment. It's only fun when not taken too seriously.

We can play at being a someone. There's transcendence involved here. But who is "we"? There is always an assumed someone, it seems, and transcendence is a ceaseless dialectic—certainly beyond logic and maybe even time. We can imagine or experience the non-dual only because we remain dual. Self is essentially dualistic, and self is required if we wish to think and experience life. This is why I believe no-self means no-fixed-self.

This is intended as descriptive of an actual experience, of course, and not simply as an idea. Can one actually realize this? I, at least, cannot say for sure. I can only testify that the exercise (play) of attempting to do so yields some interesting and enjoyably incremental results. How does one attempt to realize it? Again, I can only speak of my own practice—imaginative meditation.

Clinging to a fixed-identity—one that can be lost and must forever be protected and propped up—let's call it an egoic-self—a self trapped in itself—is mostly just a bad habit. Self is an evolved habit—not an evil—just what's happened. There's no need to disparage it. But nor is there any reason why we shouldn't wish to improve upon its performance when some aspects of it prove dysfunctional. Nothing's perfect. Nothing's "meant" to be. Imaginative meditation amounts to the consideration of other possible, more beneficial habits—new ways of thinking and being. It entails venturing forth into new experiences—mystical experiences.

Imagination takes place in the spirit of play. Nothing need be taken as "real"—it's all just having fun because that's the best we can do, and fun is fun. Religious-mindedness is taking things far too seriously, and that is the death of fun.

XIII

It seems logical enough to assume there can be no identity without existence, but can there be existence without identity? Is there existence without identity when there is no mind to think it? Probably; but it's hard, if not impossible, for the mind to think it. Even so-called Non-Being and non-existence seem to have existence. Where there is thought, everything thought has an assigned identity. The "problem" of identity seems to be a creation of the discriminating mind.

This is a rock; and more than that, it is this specific rock, my pet rock. Previously, it was part of a boulder, and had no such identity. What does this tell me of its present identity? In the future, it will likely become many smaller rocks, sand, dust, atoms, and..? What will have become of its present identity? Shall I mourn the future loss of this rock? Or can I instead imagine identity as a non-essential attribute somewhat more aligned with hardness or density so that its loss does not affect its continuity? I can't; but I can learn something in the attempt.

Might I just as well mourn that it previously had no identity? What's the difference between its previously not having been this rock and its future ceasing to be this rock? Why do I mourn my own likely loss of identity and not that I once had none? Who says I have an identity in any case? I do.

Are we really any different than this rock? Cosmically speaking, we are not. But wait! *I* most certainly am! The loss of my own identity is something I do not wish to entertain, cosmic perspectives notwithstanding. I must be an exception. Perhaps I am an eternal soul (at least going forward; going backward seems a bit more problematical). Or maybe there's just One Identity, I AM, and that's me (and you, too, if you wish). Whew! I feel better already.

Whatever "solution" we might devise to deal with the probable loss of our identity in death, it's clear that we want one. "I haven't a clue" is probably the most honest response. This leads Zhuangzi to suggest we "just hand it all over to the unavoidable"—in thankfulness and trust. No theory is going to change reality, in any case. But he also dabbles a bit is his own imaginative solution. Since Transformation seems the universal way of things, why not simply identify with that? One with Change, what change could harm you? But this requires breaking our addiction to fixed-identity—identity as the essential, rather than as accidental. It requires imagining a kind continuity completely innocent of identity. This is his no-fixed-identity—an experience that can only occur beyond the deliberating mind that cannot dispense with identity.

This "solution" led Fang Yizhi (1611-1671) to accuse Zhuangzi of "cooking up his own pot of Buddha-flesh" (p 170)—dodging his own existential dangle. There could be some truth in this, but if we grant Zhuangzi the possibility of consistency, then his imaginative solution can be understood as but another self-aware coping strategy, and not a representation of the truth of things.

COSMO-CENTRISM AND ENVIRONMENTAL JUSTICE
I – XI

I

I have suggested that philosophical Daoism's imaginative exercise in the equalization of all things creates a cosmo-centrism that issues in a deep sense of environmental concern. Several clarifications are in order before we proceed further in an investigation of how this is so.

Foremost, it needs to be reiterated that this is a *psychological* exercise and not a statement of how things "really" are. It also assumes more than mere intellectual assent; it assumes a transformative experience. Nothing need be "true" for its imagined possibility to issue in an experienced recontextualization, a paradigm shift. You don't have to get it right to get it. Where every world-view is imagined in any case, this is not outside the norm.

By cosmo-centrism I mean a point of view that so identifies with the cosmos that all it contains shares in our natural self-love. "Heaven and earth were born together with me, and all things and I are one." (2:32) My body is all bodies. There is one body.

As a hierarchy of concerns the trajectory is reversible, though not commensurate. On the human plane self-flourishing (dialectically) precedes species-, environmental-, and cosmic-flourishing. We begin with our self-care and that informs our care for others. On the "higher" plane cosmic-flourishing precedes the rest. Yet we only work up from the human plane and never down from the cosmic-plane because cosmic-flourishing is taken as an unconditional given. All is and will be well whatever temporal outcomes might transpire. No need for cosmic-redemption is imagined.

This "work" entails both an active concern for the flourishing of all things and the exercise of the wisdom that justly makes the compromises that the exigencies of existence require. We honor the mountain even as we take its ore, should that ore be deemed necessary to our collective-flourishing. Yet honoring the mountain requires its preservation as best as possible.

II

In the context of Zhuangzian philosophy further clarification of the idea and experience of cosmo-centrism seems necessary in as much as it casts us into the middle of his disagreements with his friend, the Logician Huizi.

Huizi believed that he had logically (albeit, paradoxically) demonstrated the oneness of things: "Love all things without exception, for heaven and earth are one body." (33; p 124) Zhuangzi took Huizi to task, not for this conclusion as is often averred, but because it went no further than intellectual assent. Zhuangzi suggested a mystical leap as the necessary next step. Huizi preferred to dwell solely in the world of intellection and for this reason called Zhuangzi's philosophy "big and useless".

When, after presenting some of his own paradoxes, Zhuangzi exclaims, "Heaven and earth are born together with me, and the ten thousand things and I are one" (2:32), he means it. (Many scholars take this as an ironic dig at Huizi, but I believe they are mistaken.) He means it, not in a literal (logically proven) sense, but in an experiential sense. He probably just experienced it.

Such an experience, at least as a temporary ecstatic moment, is not difficult to realize. All one needs to do is imaginatively engage with Zhuangzi's own paradoxes and take the leap they invite: "Nothing in the world is larger than the tip of a hair in autumn, and Mt. Tai is small. No one lives longer than a dead child, and old Pengzu died young." Alternatively, one can simply meditatively imagine the equalization of all things.

Though such a "buzz" is admittedly superficial, still it provides an inkling of the possibility of a deeper, more organic experience. Our cosmo-centrism, our identification with the Totality, will necessarily be and likely remain a work in progress. Our practical engagement vis-à-vis the environment will follow apace. Our continued flourishing as a species will likely depend on it.

III

Cosmo-centrism is the ability to care for all things as an extension of one's natural care for oneself. "Others", whether that be people, animals, plants, or inanimate things, do not exist for my sake (ego-centrism) or for the sake of humanity (species-centrism), or ultimately even for the sake of the Cosmos (yes, Cosmo-centrism), but for themselves—just like you and I do.

All things are to themselves as I am to myself. All things are my-selves. All things are myself. All things are loved even as we self-love.

Ziporyn's "omnicentrism" is another way of imagining this. Everything is the center. Everything contextualizes ("explains") everything else (just like you do). Yet nothing is the exclusive center, since all things are the center. This is a Oneness that in no way prejudices the inviolability of the Many; there is One only in and through the Many. And like most anything that seems to get at the un-gettable-ness of existence, it is paradoxical—or nonsensical, if you prefer.

The Cosmos is much more than the totality of things, however. It is much more than a thing in itself. It is that outside of which nothing can be imagined. Since we cannot imagine this, it must fail as a designation. It is ultimately empty. As such it is open-ended. Cosmo-centrism is thus also openness.

Openness here means that when we imagine the cosmos we also take it as Mystery. Our minds do not close around a concept, but remain open and unfixed. The mind remains "released to play in the harmony of all *de*", all expressions of Dao.

It is this openness that enables a Cosmo-centrism, an appreciation of the oneness of things that does not prejudice things in their individual self-so uniqueness. "Not-one is also One."

Our projects of self-and world-improvement are thus always informed by their embedding in the context of Mystery which requires no improvement.

IV

The phrase "environmental justice" already implies the self-so value of the planet. It has rights. Everything on it has rights. Planetary rights are not human rights; those rights must be informed by the rights of all other things. Saving the planet to save ourselves has motivational merit, but cosmo-centrism motivates a more fundamental sense of justice. The planet has its own rights irrespective of its utility to humanity.

This sense alone encourages a significant paradigm shift. It impacts our ego-centrism. When Ziqi lost his "me" this is the kind of recontextualization he experienced. All the forest's trees have their own unique voices in response to the same wind, yet "each selects out its own". (2:5) Each one is self-so—self-arising and inherently valuable. (If my existence has value, then every existence has value, without exception. This is the equalization of things.)

Which comes first, the loss of one's "me", or this sense of cosmo-centrism? They likely dialectically inform each other. For my part, meditation on the "illuminated obvious" equality of all beings serves as a gateway to a realization of the possible loss of my "me". This "inkling" has efficacy where dialectical approximation is the actual real-world circumstance.

The promise of meditatively realizing that loss as Ziqi hypothetically did (it *is* just a story, after all), though worthy of pursuit, needn't obviate the need for the real-time, practical exercise of that outcome irrespective of meditative "success". Not only do we not need to get it right to get it, neither do we need to get it to do what's right.

Practicing environmental justice is thus itself an act of self-cultivation. Exercising a sense of cosmo-centrism in one's interface with the world impacts one's relationship with one's self-experience. If one's "me" is not lost, as in Ziqi's meditative ideal, at least it is being approximatingly recontextualized.

It's a win-win.

V

The call for environmental justice implies that injustices have already been committed. We have abused this planet. We have essentially taken it as there *for* us. We have engaged in species-centrism in the extreme.

And now we realize that our abuse of the planet has become a form of self-abuse. Our own survival, or at least flourishing, is at risk. We now understand that we must "save" the planet in order to save ourselves. Yet this motivation remains within the spheres of species- and ego-centrism—attitudes that significantly contributed to the problem in the first place. If we are to really break the cycle, we need a radical paradigm shift.

That shift is what I'm calling cosmo-centrism, the recontextualization of our ego- and species-centrism within the broader context of the (ultimately ambiguous) world-context.

Cosmo-centrism embraces two apparently mutually exclusive experiences. On the one hand, it recognizes the absolute non-negotiable value of each and every thing in its individual uniqueness. On the other hand, it so completely identifies with the world that it is taken as one body—my body, your body. Together these views issue in an equality of caring.

This is walking the two roads of not-oneness and oneness at the same time. Wholly identifying with the world as one body illuminates the equality of value of the many. Appreciating the self-so value of the many is seeing their oneness. They are all the same in their all being different.

"For belonging in a category [similar] and not belonging in that category [different] themselves form another category [similar]! Being similar is so similar to being dissimilar!" exclaims Zhuangzi. (2:30) Even the category "One" invites another category. This renders it empty of all true content and returns us to openness in the presence of Mystery.

VI

We might do well to understand something of the origins of our present predominant world-view so as to better understand the radical nature of the paradigm shift philosophical Daoism advocates.

First and foremost I think we need to realize that this self-destructive world-view is entirely natural, just as we recognize the ego-self as a product of human evolution, despite its inherent problems.

Let's stay with this for a moment, for it is a statement of momentous importance. This isn't about right and wrong. It's about what has arisen; and that always comes with problems. Existence is an extremely messy business. It behooves us to come to grips with the lack of any discernable normative and purposive principle in the arising of things. Things apparently just happen.

Ego- and species-centrism are entirely natural inclinations; and they have significantly contributed to the survival and flourishing of our species. Evolution, however, implies that improvements are always necessarily in the offing. What was previously beneficial might not be so in the future. Multitudes of species have evolved into existential cul-de-sacs and have consequentially perished in their failure to change apace with environmental circumstances. Humanity has now reached such a crossroad.

What seems unique about humanity is that it has evolved the ability to take control of its own temporal circumstances. Humanity can evolve because and as humanity wills it. Our next evolutionary step—hopefully a revolution in consciousness—may very well be a chosen one.

The onus of responsibility rests entirely on us. No manifest destiny, no "true purpose", no species-exceptionalism written in the heavens will guarantee our survival. For Nature, we are of no greater value than the species, worlds and universes already extinct. It's up to us; if we are up to the challenge.

Realizing that we are not special could become one of the most special things about us. It might very well be a first among things.

VII

Our default ego- and species-centrism have naturally arisen. Their unquestioned perpetuation, however, has become a matter of cultural programming. Though I think it can be demonstrated that this is largely true of every religious expression (when we look at behavior rather than words), this is especially the case with the three "great" monotheistic religions.

The belief that the world is there for our use is an ineluctable derivative of the Judeo-Christian-Islamic creation myth. God created the world for himself, and it exists solely for his pleasure. Sentient beings fulfil this purpose through worship, bringing "glory to God".

This is the fundamental template by which we order our own relationship with Nature. Created "in the image of God", we are his earthly surrogates. We are exhorted to go into all the world and "subdue" it. We are a special species within creation ("a little lower than the angels" (Heb. 2:7)), and it exists *for* us to use as we wish. The idea of "stewardship" is the only accommodation toward environmental concern that this can offer, yet it remains species-centric.

Man's first task was to "name all the animals". Naming them, we own them. They are objectified through language and as such become wholly other than ourselves and objects for our manipulation.

Woman was an afterthought—man was lonely. She is there *for* man, his "helpmate"—the help. She, too, is to be subdued.

It is easy to see how millennia of this and other similar creation myths have reinforced our natural inclination toward species-and ego-centrism. They have divine sanction. Indeed, they are mandated.

Clearly the radical paradigm shift required to transform our relationship with Nature will require moving beyond our formative myths. It's past time to grow up. It's time for Humanity 2.0.

VIII

Daoist cosmology, to the extent it can be said to have one, is altogether different than the Creator/creation myth. "Dao does nothing, yet nothing is left undone." (*Laozi* 37) Things just happen—or so it seems. There is no known manipulation involved in their arising. No mediating purposiveness is implied. Things arise for themselves alone. They are self-so. This is their equality, and a condition of our cosmo-centrism.

Dao does nothing because it is neither a something nor a nothing; it is present as an absence.

Daoists are encouraged to live similarly. *Wu-wei*, not-doing, is the emulation of this fundamental ("obvious") attribute of apparent world-arising. If things just happen, and we affirm that happening, then we do best to let them happen.

Our letting them happen, however, paradoxically helps them to happen in a certain way. We are present in our absence. We influence from a distance and by way of distance. *Wu-wei* is not indifference, but a strategy for change. It is not being the change (manipulatively), but non-being the change. It is yin-ing in the world of yang.

The planetary bio-sphere is in danger as a consequence of human activity. Science wants to fix it. Radical geo-engineering projects have been suggested. Release aerosols into the atmosphere. Dump iron into the oceans. What could possibly go wrong? Isn't this just more of the same, with potentially even greater negative consequences?

Science can and does also sometimes practice *wu-wei*. Illuminating the problem is itself a non-coercive contribution to remedying the problem. It creates the motivational space for change to happen. Understanding how the environment can heal itself and allowing it to do so is possible. Not-doing what we have been doing is also the practice of *wu-wei*.

Environmental justice is ultimately about allowing all things to self-flourish—something they do quite naturally without the help of our "stewardship". Cosmo-centrism is the organic sense that we are all in this together and thus that the moderation of our own wants actually contributes to our own self-flourishing.

THE INDIFFERENCE OF BIRDS

IX

Though we might understand the equality of all things and engage in a cosmo-centric caring, still there remains a hierarchy of caring. One's self-flourishing trumps the flourishing of the food on one's plate. Our need for shelter trumps the need of the tree to fully live out its years.

As always, we are cast into ambiguity. We have not arrived at a pat formula by which we can live in the simple application of a principle. We must make informed choices; though the wisdom of no choice is guaranteed. Yet wisdom it is that is required.

Some of that wisdom is an appreciation of simplicity. What do we actually need? What can be legitimately sacrificed to those needs? The mega-yacht, personal airliner, or even luxury car, is a choice to ignore the needs of others for the ego-centric pleasure of conspicuous consumption, is it not?

Though extreme in their position, the so-called Primitivist Chapters of the *Zhuangzi* (8-11a) speak to the destruction of things for the sake of ego-and species-centrism. "Unless the white jade is broken, what can be made into the ritual scepters and batons?... The mutilation of the unhewn raw material to make valued vessels is the crime of the skilled carpenter." (9; p 62)

If this is so, then we are all criminals. Yet such a criminality is an unavoidable attribute of the existence of any one thing. In this regard it is helpful to remember Zhuangzi's equalizing unification of formation and destruction: "Whenever fragmentation is going on, formation, completion, is also going on. Whenever formation is going on, destruction is also going on. Hence, all things are neither formed nor destroyed, for these two also open into each other, connecting to form a oneness." (2:21-2) Ultimately, nothing is lost. We need fear no prosecution.

This required wisdom is much more than practical knowledge: "Much wisdom in the use of traps, nets, snares, and lattices throws the beasts of the woodlands into disorder... Thus it is that each and every great disorder of the world is caused by the love of wisdom." (10; p 65)

Yet, there is a "wisdom that is free of wisdom" (4:30); it is the wisdom that questions itself: "Everyone in the world knows how to raise questions about what they don't know, but none know how to raise questions about what they already know. Everyone knows enough to reject what they consider bad, but not enough to reject what they consider good. This is the reason for the great disorder, which violates the brightness of the sun and moon above and melts away the vital essence of the mountains and rivers below, toppling the ordered succession of the four seasons in between." (10; p 66)

A prophetic word to be sure.

X

Though Daoist sagacity is, to my thinking, only an ideal, still it can be incrementally approximated. Among the attributes of a sage are those which embody the attitudes and behaviors that allow for world-flourishing.

I have already mentioned simplicity as one of these attitudes. The root of true simplicity lays in the eradication of the self-reifying project. Wanting to "be somebody", we are further motivated to acquire the accoutrements of perceived "success". This equates to the pursuit of "fame" (name—self- and other-perceived) through the accumulation of wealth and power and the conspicuous consumption that they allow.

The sage, having lost her "me", has no-fixed-identity and thus no self that requires external support. She depends on nothing for her sense of self-worth. She is self-so. She is free to wander in her selfhood while allowing others to do the same. She has abandoned the zero-sum game. Her self-worth does not require the diminishment of the worth of others, human or otherwise.

Ideally, simplicity need not be practiced; it organically arises; it happens. In the real world, however, practice is necessary. We can practice simplicity as a work of self-cultivation and simultaneously lower our impact on the biosphere.

Revolutionary societal change requires a movement, and a movement requires individuals. In the end, it is individual transformation—yours and mine—that will bring about change.

Is a revolution necessary? Given the late hour and the geometrical expansion of the effects of our chronic world destruction, it would seem so. Yet still we dally.

XI

Cosmo-centrism as a paradigm shift is already in play within the environmental movement. "Deep ecology" takes it as its point of departure. Other environmental philosophies make similar reiterations of the same. How they arrived there, I am not sure; but it is encouraging that they have.

What philosophical Daoism might have to contribute to the movement are a philosophical framework for such a view and the basis for that leading to a mystical and transformative leap. In the end, mere intellectual assent, though helpful, may not be enough. What is ultimately needed is a transformation of human consciousness. And this begins with us—me and you.

This frankly leads me to pessimism. Humanity is a self- and world-abusive mess, and its inertial trajectory seems unstoppable. It is helpful to remember then that the planet does not require saving at all. It will do quite well without us however we leave it, thank you very much. It has survived a lot worse than us.

Nor do *we* ultimately require saving, for that matter. Our collective extinction is as assured as our individual deaths. Nothing ultimately requires saving, because nothing *can* be saved. But then, by the same token, nothing can be lost. This, too, is open-ended cosmo-centrism, "the vastest arrangement" in which all things are secured beyond the sense of identity.

Informed by this, we can get on with the work of caring with a hope that is also not-hope, a hope that requires no particular outcome.

Heal the sick,
Though they shall die in the end.
Fix what is broken,
Though it shall surely break again.
Do all that you must,
Yet remain forever at rest.
  —Chen Jen

I WANT TO BE A SAGE
I – XV

I

There are innumerable personal failings that I could share with the reader, but none as illuminating or seminal as this: I want to be a sage.

For the most part I try to avoid being overly personal in these posts; they are not meant to be about me, but about the applicability of the philosophy of Zhuangzi to life today. That applicability, however, does not and cannot come disembodied from a life experience, and the only one I know is my own. Alas, this entire project is about me. On the one hand, it grieves me to have to say so; on the other, I realize that there is no other option and that any pretense of disinterested objectivity in anything amounts to an act of bad faith—to lie to oneself and to others.

Zhuangzi's project was no different. We have this in common—we are both human. He too was simply trying to cope with his experience and, I believe, *knew* this to be the case. *That* critical self-awareness is the hinge upon which his philosophy can be said to turn.

For me, Daoism is an entirely psychological project. It has nothing to do with a supposed extra-mundane Reality except as a Lack. We *feel* that it is necessary, yet can only *feel* it as a lack. And so too do we experience ourselves as a lack; something is missing, and it's the most important thing of all. Let the coping begin.

This being a psychological project, there is much to discover in self-inquiry. There is no other place *to* begin—or to end. I have mentioned my desire to be a sage as one point of entry into such an inquiry. Exploring this will take more than one post, so, in the interest of suggesting at least a modicum of supposed sagacity (because I want to be a sage), let me begin by saying that this does not mean that I want to be a guru surrounded by adoring disciples. This inquiry will be an exploration of ever-deeper and more subtle motivations, and the desire to be such a guru is on the peripheral first ring, and the coarsest of possible motivations. It is not one I generally entertain. I'd rather be a rock star. This has the advantage of indulging in a self-reifying fantasy without the hypocrisy.

II

I have offered my personal *failing* of desiring to be a sage as a point of entry into the necessary self-inquiry that Zhuangzi's philosophy challenges us to practice. That philosophy begins and ends in our self-experience. It's about the transformation of our world-view, our interface with our personal experience in the world, and nothing else. It is not a belief system, but a self-aware existential response to the life-experience as it arises. It makes no appeal to extra-mundane metaphysical "realities".

I have said I'd rather be a rock star than an adored guru. The implication is that to aspire to either manifests more or less the same motivation. Understanding how they are the same is vital to understanding the Zhuangzian project of realizing non-dependence and the freedom to play and wander. The essence of non-dependence is the loss of the need to "be someone". When he says, "Just be empty", this is what he means. Being who we are is, ironically, being no one. We are, of course, "someone"; we are a someone who is also a no one. Our core experience, Zhuangzi suggests, is a sense of emptiness. We are not a *thing*, a concrete, static entity, but a *happening*, an expression of a ceaseless, open-ended transformation.

This disturbs us. We want to be someone fixed. We want to be gods, concrete and immortal. For this reason, we engage in all manner of self-reifying fantasies and projects in an attempt to fill the unfillable core emptiness that is our essential experience.

This desire to be a rock star (or an adored guru) is motivated by a desire to be esteemed by others in the extreme, though it is of the same genus as every similar motivation. It is, as I have said, the coarsest of such motivations and one easily identified and condemned. But condemnation is not abandonment, and for that, there's nothing so effective as laughter. Laughter, however, neither condemns nor abandons; it simply joyously transcends and leaves things to transform as they may.

Self-laughter is an active self-awareness that is already free of that of which it is aware. While self-inquiry is a project of self-cultivation, self-laughter is the freedom that simultaneously obviates any requirement for change. It is the realization of complete unconditional self-affirmation in each moment and in every condition. It is the caged bird that sings—even as it works on the bars.

III

The desire to "be someone" motivates pretty much everything we do in terms of our interface with ourselves and the world. This is what makes the concept of emptiness so incredibly difficult to envision and to realize. Yet emptiness is not intended as a negation—what's there to negate? If there were a real "fixed-self" (or a "true self", for that matter) then we would do better to affirm and be it. Our actual experience, however, indicates otherwise. We are perpetually *trying* to be someone because at our deepest core we experience ourselves as a no one. Emptiness then is an affirmation of who we "are", not its negation. There is no evil self to eradicate.

None of this futile, self-reifying project would matter all that much except in that it tends to diminish our own enjoyment of life and that of others. No cosmic consequences obtain. Neither we nor the cosmos require saving. *Humpty-Dumpty* (*hundun*, primordial chaos) does not yearn to be put back together again. The pursuit of our individual and collective flourishing need not be a religious project.

Because we are nearly always motivated by a desire to be someone in our interface with ourselves and others does not mean that what we do is to be negated. Our motivations can cast a shadow on our actions, but the actions themselves can remain affirmable. Saving Mencius' child about to fall into a well remains commendable whether it is accomplished so as to be seen as "good", or as a natural expression of empathy, as Mencius would have it. It is likely to be both.

Wanting to be a sage is likely to be overshadowed by motivations that are themselves a negation of sagacity, but the pursuit of sagacity remains a worthy project nonetheless. Yet, here we have the paradox common to all such endeavors: one cannot become a sage while wanting to be a sage; one does not become a buddha by trying to be a buddha; one cannot be happy through the pursuit of happiness. What then are we to do? The best we can do is to be human—to live and work within the contingencies of our inherently messy experience. In this is the possibility of proximally realizing what is likely only an unobtainable ideal. Living *that* is sagacious freedom.

IV

The desire to *be seen as* a sage is the desire to be esteemed by others. Not surprisingly, we find ourselves back on the track of Zhuangzi's brief but potent examination of forms of dependence from the coarsest to the most subtle. He concludes by telling us that the sage has no-self, which I take to mean that she has experientially understood the emptiness of the self-experience. This uncovering of levels of motivational dependence (of which he provides three) invites us to discover them in ourselves so as to realize freedom from them.

He begins with a critique of someone who takes political (social) status as somehow capable of bringing fulfilment to one's life. This is likely an allusion to his sparring buddy Huizi who did in fact mange to become a political someone in one of the warring states. This political person is also likened to the tiny dove who scoffs at the incredible flight of the vast bird Peng which is again likely an allusion to Huizi who criticized Zhuangzi's philosophy as big, but useless. All this *is* about Zhuangzi, lest we forget. I take him to be an existentialist and phenomenologist (one who describes experience without reference to presupposed causes) very much like Kierkegaard—take away the personal, and nothing remains.

Have we then sufficiently uncovered this form of motivational dependence? Not quite. The desire to be a rock star guru is easily dismissed as ridiculously egoic. There are, however, more subtle and insidious expressions of this desire for the esteem of others. A recent experience of one of these gave birth to this series. I have a friend who calls me "my Master"—entirely ironically it needs to be said, his mess being in many ways less than my own. He had occasion to chide me for my anger and impatience at difficulties encountered while doing a boat project. I became angry at his criticism. This ruined my day. And I wanted to know why.

The reason pertinent to this topic of dependence on the esteem of others is simply that, though I knew he knew I was a mess, I did not want that he should have more evidence of the fact. I was unhappy because I felt diminished in the eyes of another. This amply demonstrates the value of *not* depending on the esteem of others. If one's happiness depends on *any*thing, then one will never be happy. Zhuangzian wandering is just this: being happy in every circumstance, even unhappy ones.

It needs to be said that growing in patience, though a worthy project, has nothing to do with growing in non-dependence. If we require ourselves to become "better", we are dependent on that and the same bondage obtains. This is a moral stumbling-block for many who see it as a shirking of responsibility, but it need be no such thing where one walks two roads at once.

V

After exposing the folly of pursuing the esteem of *others*, Zhuangzi considers the desire for *self*-esteem. We are told that *even* the proto-Daoist Song Xing would laugh at someone who attempts to be someone through social-esteem. There seems to be lots of laughing going on here. The tiny dove laughs at the flight of the vast bird Peng—*derisively*. Song Xing laughs at the one who, like the dove, sees himself in comparison to others. One ancient commentator points out that Zhuangzi says "even Song Xing" because, though he had some insight into the folly of self-reifying at that level, he had yet to learn to laugh at himself. Ostensibly, Zhuangzi's sage has realized the freedom to do just that.

Song Xing, we are told (by Zhuangzi and the author of the 33rd chapter of the *Zhuangzi*), clearly recognized the difference between the inner and the outer. He understood the latter, dependence on the esteem of others, to be oppressive. Instead, he suggested we nurture the inner, our self-esteem. Song proclaimed that "to be insulted is not a disgrace"—it need not bother us. What a wonderful concept! What a powerful invitation to explore the root causes for our typical responses to an insult. Why does it upset us? Shouldn't we be so self-esteeming that the opinions of others have no affect? This is about as far as self-help psychology can take us and is likely a helpful, remedial project, though Zhuangzi suggests we can take it yet further.

Ziporyn describes this as "a salutary first step". It is a significant insight and worthy of consideration and *practice*. For this, I would suggest, is the kind of "practice" that Zhuangzi suggests—the hard work of understanding ourselves. Meditation might have a role to play, but it can easily simply feed the same egoic motivations that Zhuangzi suggests we uncover and illuminate so as to transcend them—laugh at them.

Know thyself. Yet when the Emperor of China asked the putative first patriarch of Chan (Zen), Bodhidharma, who the hell did he think he was, he replied, I don't know. Now *that's* knowing oneself.

VI

Dependence on the esteem of others and dependence on one's self-esteem are expressions of the same desire to be someone, though moving from the former to the latter would be a commendable accomplishment. It's likely, however, that where there is the one, there is the other. For the purposes of his argument, Zhuangzi assumes that, because Song Xing advocated for a self-esteem freed from a dependence on the esteem of others, he had actually realized it. I think it unlikely, just as I think it unlikely that any of these so-called masters actually realized the visions to which they aspired. This is more than just consistent with Zhuangzi's philosophy; it is pivotal to it. Nothing is complete and final; nothing is fixed and sure. When something is taken as complete, something is left out; and that something necessarily becomes the most important thing of all. A belief in fully-realized sages and "masters" is the provenance of the religious-mind, a mind that requires (depends on) the fixed and sure.

When I say I want to be a sage it is largely a matter of wanting to see myself as such. I want to be a sage so I can feel good about myself. Though this also entails wishing to be seen as a sage by others, the chief motivation is self-esteem. Real self-esteem is likely more easily achieved by some than by others. Who of the two would more likely wish to depend on no esteem at all? Remedial projects are motivated by perceived need; though probably universally applicable, they need not be universally prescribed.

Zhuangzi makes his case for the virtues of realizing freedom from dependence on absolutely everything, and he does so through a phenomenological investigation of his own experience. Free of

69

dependence, we are free to wander in every circumstance. "Just release the mind to play..." He believes that this investigation of his own experience also illuminates the human condition generally. In this sense it is prescriptive. Yet, since he understands his dao to be just another dao, and because his dao sees Dao as the confluence of all daos, he is not dogmatically prescriptive. The contented self-esteemer (should there be such a one), or anyone else, for that matter, is fully affirmed as they are, and left to choose any dao they wish. People typically choose a measure of misery given the cost of freedom (no-self—being a nobody), and frankly, the difficulties of actually realizing it. Who are we to fault them?

IV

Zhuangzi suggests three increasingly subtle expressions of our ceaseless project of trying to be someone. This project is a consequence of the core emptiness that pulls the rug out from under our desire to be substantive and eternal. Since this is an entirely futile exercise and one that creates a pall of disharmony with ourselves, others, and the cosmos, he recommends that we rather harmonize with our actual experience. Everything is ceaselessly transforming; identify with that, and we need no longer cling to something we fear we can lose. Or don't; it's just a life-strategy, a dao, not "the Dao".

What typically motivates this project of realizing one's inherent emptiness? Taking ourselves as someone, we seek to be no one as a means to being someone. The so-called "spiritual" project becomes just another expression of the self-reifying project. This, I think, is what Zhuangzi intends to convey when he offers Liezi's spiritual accomplishments as his final example of dependence. Liezi could fly on the wind. That's quite an accomplishment; but, Zhuangzi tells us, this is still an expression of dependence.

Some Daoist roots likely extend deep into shamanism, and Liezi (if he existed) might very well have been more shamanist than "Daoist". Shamanism offers an excellent example of a self-reifying form of "spirituality". I do not mean to imply that it is more so than other forms—there are no spiritual pursuits that do not also have their self-reifying expressions—, but rather that some of its overt peculiarities make it easily identifiable as such. (What do I know of shamanism? I have only opinions.) Shamanism is very much about "spiritual" power. Castaneda's Don Juan is a shaman. We are invited to be amazed at how much spiritual power he has—he could astral-project. Wow. Ask an aspiring shamanist about her shaman guru and she will tell you of his powers. You too can have such powers. You too can be someone special. None of this is meant to disparage shamanism, but simply to illustrate how Zhuangzi saw his project as something altogether different.

But Zhuangzi's pursuit of non-dependent wandering can just as easily be a self-reifying project. The real question is whether it could possibly be anything else. It might be helpful to fall back on the Buddhist conundrum: you can't become a buddha by trying to be a buddha, yet you are obliged to keep trying until you somehow need try no more. We stand on the bank of our essential mess, and look across the uncrossable river in the belief that we can vaguely discern the other side. This has remedial benefit to be sure. But we also need to remember that process is the most authentic goal, and that process is of necessity a messy business. If we are able to embrace the non-logical infinite regress of wandering in our inability to wander, or to wander in our inability to do even that... then we can perhaps make proximal "progress" and wander in the doing.

VIII

This series is supposed to be overtly about me, yet in having fallen into the familiar groove of Zhuangzi's analysis of dependence, it has sometimes become only covertly so. I somewhat ashamedly suggested early on, however, that this must of necessity be about me whether acknowledged or not. Such is the nature of being human. Even the astrophysicist in the spin of her theories is speaking about herself. Pure objectivity is a myth. This, in any case, is what Zhuangzi suggests when he says that every point of view is indeed from a specific point, and that there are as many points as there are people viewing from them.

Kierkegaard suggested that "truth is subjectivity" which I take to mean that, despite the admittedly objective side of a statement of the truth of things, it necessarily requires a subjective commitment to it. It is not truth until someone says it is. ("Things are 'so' because someone says they are 'so'", as Zhuangzi puts it.) One must cast one's lot into the truthfulness of a truth. But this "leap" is not entirely logically justifiable—in the end, nothing is entirely "provable".

Kierkegaard was most concerned with Christianity, of course. In his native Denmark (part of "Christendom") everyone was a "Christian"; when everyone is a Christian, he averred, no one is a Christian. Being a Christian involves a personal existential leap of faith into the absurdity of taking something as absolutely True—not being part of a herd. It's not God becoming a man that is so absurd (an idea), but that the guy over there shitting behind a bush *is* that man (a fact).

Zhuangzi, I would suggest, also understands that truth is subjectivity, but directs his leap in an altogether different and, I think, more authentic direction. He leaps into the human life-experience itself which, from the point of view of reason, is an absolutely absurdity. Ziporyn's rendering of Zhuangzi puts it succinctly: "Thus, the Radiance of Drift and Doubt is the sage's only map." The sage leaps into the "illuminated obvious" and lives and wanders in unknowing uncertainty. She embraces her adriftedness and playfully drifts without leaping into any particular absurdity at all.

Of course, life is only absurd to the rationalist—it doesn't make sense. This is ironic in that it is often the supposedly non-rationalist existentialists who call life absurd—it doesn't meet their rational expectations. Life is not an *ab*surdity, but a surd—it does not resolve to logic.

IX

Having suggested three increasingly subtle levels of dependence, Zhuangzi next asks how it would be to depend on nothing. Why, wouldn't we be able to soar upon every possible circumstance? An insult would mean nothing; "failure" wouldn't affect our inner peace any more than would "success"; the exercise of spiritual power might happen, but would have nothing to do with our sense of worth, "spiritual" or otherwise.

He poses this as a hypothetical. He only invites us to imagine such a possibility. If we were to take it as a fixed goal to be attained, wouldn't that just set the stage for more dependence? If I wanted to be a sage, I'd want to be other than I am; I'd be dependent on certain outcomes; I'd judge myself according to predetermined expectations. I'd still be on the treadmill.

Here I must (again) repeat myself. There is a dialectic here that is very difficult to describe. It's a perpetual self-effacement that effaces nothing. We aspire to sagacity while not-aspiring to sagacity, while aspiring to sagacity... This is an infinite regress of willing and not-willing, wanting and not wanting—affirming and negating. Isn't this really just a reflection of the life-experience itself? Hope dawns eternal—life is a ceaseless series of disappointments and renewals of hope, because life is a perpetual élan. Life is becoming. Being is becoming. Becoming what? Nothing in particular; just becoming. Pure becoming has no fixed point of departure and no known end. "True-self" has no home here, except as its own self-effacement.

Why then do Zhuangzi's most immediate interpreters begin speaking of a "true-self" and an "innate nature"? Because we want to *be someone*, to be *substantive*, and realizing ourselves as nobody is the last thing we want to do.

Zhuangzian non-dependence, it needs to be said, has nothing to do with *in*dependence. Quite to the contrary; it is because we are utterly dependent in every way that we can realize a psychological non-dependence through identification with the Great Becoming. All is transformation; in identifying with Transformation, what transformations can affect us? In identifying with Change, what changes can disturb us? No-one has nothing to lose.

X

In the final analysis, wanting to be a sage is wanting to be someone. Yet, the hypothetical sage is no one. What are we to do? We can be this contradiction. We can be this mess. We can wander in precisely that place in which we find ourselves. We can depend on the realization of nothing—including this... and this... If we can't wander in our not-wandering, then we are unlikely to ever wander—for wandering is non-dependence, even on wandering.

Why is a sage no one? Because everyone is no one. This, at any rate, is what Zhuangzi concludes when he "illuminates the obvious", when he considers his life-experience phenomenologically, just as it manifests, without the imposition of essentialist myths. When Yan practiced "fasting of the mind" he discovered that he had "yet to begin to exist" (4:10). He saw with his inner qi. What is qi? Emptiness. Becoming. The "space" in which things happen. There's nothing substantial there. He experienced no bolt from Above. No union with some Ultimate *thing* took place. He did not realize the Great Dao. He did not become "spiritual". He was not "enlightened". He didn't find his "true purpose". "I AM" was not substantiated. The Cosmos was not illuminated. No one was saved.

Zhuangzi might be full of shit (I certainly am), but to my thinking, we at least owe him the courtesy of allowing him to speak without casting him into the mold of his religious-minded interpreters, ancient or modern.

XI

Zhuangzi concludes his case for non-dependence with his most definitive statement on the nature of a sage: "Thus I say, the Consummate Person has no fixed-identity, the Spirit Man has no particular merit, the Sage has no name" (1:8).

This is apparently what I want to be when I grow up; but I gave up on that project long ago. But wait, maybe there's a distant similarity between the two. Admittedly, most "giving up" remains squarely in the realm of "failure" (though little more so than "not giving up"). But isn't there a Zenny guy who was "enlightened" at just such a moment? Indeed, isn't "giving up" a necessary precursor to satori?

Let's begin with some de-mythologizing of this sentence. None of these subjects require capitalization. Such non-grammatically required capitalization typically suggests the unique weightiness of something. A dao is just another dao; Dao is "the" Dao—the big one. (There is no capitalization in the original.) So let's return them to the lower case, and let the sage be what the sentence says she is: no one special.

But Ziporyn has a real sense of the spirit of Zhuangzi's philosophy that often makes for some very subtle (and sometimes creative) renderings. Capitalization here can also so exalt the sage as to render her a hypothetical. Hyperbolic descriptions of the sage as remaining untouched by world conflagration similarly seem to beg an act of ridiculous credulity, but can also be an occasion to break the fetters of credulity altogether. (There's method in this madness.)

Zhuangzi's *D*ao is also a hypothetical; it seems necessary, but cannot be found; it is the ever-receding incoherence that frames every attempt at coherence. It is always present as an absence, a lack. Yet without it, nothing has presence—nothing is "seen" without a background—nothing is anything without its *not being* something else. So, we can leave the sage a Sage, a big idea that functions as an insubstantial metaphorical lure—not a fixed, attainable reality—not something to believe in.

Let's also recognize that these three titles identify only one "person". Only the hyper-literal pedanticist would want to parse it otherwise. But he does us the favor of alerting us to more subtle expressions of literalism. Perfect (Consummate) person? Spirit Man? Like the one on Mt Guye who subsists on only wind and dew and flies on the backs of dragons? The Sage is the same as these, which is to say she is both hypothetically no one in her experience, and no one is reality. We will not find her; nor should we think we can be her, any more than we should think we can find "the Dao".

DISCOMBOBULATED *DE*
I – V

I

There was a man, "Shu the Discombobulated", whose body was a total mess. And yet he was *consequentially* able to not only provide for himself, but many others as well. He took in sewing and washing. He also played at divination—something about his extreme physical deformities gave him "an aura of mystical power" (*de*?). The labor-impressing government and drafting military passed him over as useless, and the former even provided him with welfare assistance—all the more to share

"A discombobulated physical form was sufficient to allow him to nourish his body, so that he was able to live out his natural life span. And how much more can be accomplished with discombobulated *de*!" (4:19)

Whatever did Zhuangzi mean by discombobulated *de*? Whatever he meant, for the discombobulated, it speaks of freedom.

What is *de*? *De* is theoretically the expression of metaphysical Dao. In this sense, all things are *de*. One cannot "stray from Dao". But it is only psychological Dao that concerns us here, and its expression is the *de* that is conditional. It can be realized or not.

One would think then that there could only be one kind of realized *de*. Yet Zhuangzi seems to contrast discombobulated *de* with other possible forms. It is an idea, after all, and on that level, he is contrasting it to other ideas of what is *de*, especially that of the Confucians.

For Confucians, she who possesses *de* is as close to perfection as one can possibly be. She is a fully realized human being. She practices *shu* (the projection of her self-caring onto the world as a whole—a form of cosmo-centrism) and its practical societal expression, *chung*. She is a really, really "good" person. *De* is a moral attribute.

Zhuangzi rejects this model. It is not the outcome he questions, however, but the motivational imposition that is thought to secure it. Trying to improve, or rather, being *required* to improve, is counter-productive. This is *wu-wei* (non-doing) in contrast to the active pursuit of the Confucian virtues (*de*) of Benevolence and Righteousness.

Discombobulated *de*, I would suggest, must therefore be, first and foremost, consciously being the *de* that we presently are; assuming we are discombobulated. I certainly am.

II

Zhuangzi's discombobulated *de*, like the physical deformities of Shu the Discombobulated, is counter-intuitively beneficial. It stands outside conventional ideas of beauty, worthiness and usefulness. In the world of yang—self-assertiveness and mediated (conditional) self-esteem—it is despised. ("The highest good is like water which benefits all the things of the world without contending with them. It dwells in the places that most men despise [low places; the swamp]." (*Laozi* 8))

If Shu's deformities actually *helped* him to live out his allotted years, how much more so might a deformed *de*? asks Zhuangzi. This apparently useless *de* is in fact most useful. As with Zhuangzi's useless trees, being of no discernible practical value, the possessor of this *de* is left alone to flourish.

Confucius, an arch Zhuangzian foil, was a conspicuous and inveterate yang-er; he wanted to transform the world through the teaching and the application of moral principle, and there was no better place to do it than among the politically powerful. This got him into more than one fix in which his life was in danger. Even in the *Analects* (18:5) there is unanswered criticism of his political ambition, and Zhuangzi himself parodies this incident (4:20).

Confucius is held up as a paragon of virtue (*de*), and rightly so—especially if we are enamored of the pursuit of conventional "goodness". And Zhuangzi? He is the eccentric uncle—an interesting character to be sure, but not really relevant to the practicalities of life. His *de* is discombobulated.

III

"Only an insect can be an insect, and it is only by being an insect that it can succeed in being the Heavenly." (23; p 102) Being the "Heavenly" is being what we are. This is *de*. Discombobulated *de* is being the mess that we most likely are.

Being what we are sounds tautological—how could we do otherwise? Getting that sense in which we cannot be otherwise, for all its connotations of determinism, can paradoxically be quite liberating. But there is also that sense in which we can psychologically be other than we are.

(This tends toward the metaphysical, so let's first establish that it is only an imaginative exercise.)

"I am perfect by virtue of my being perfectly who I am." This mantra simply expresses an all-affirming appreciation of the Great Happening. Every happening, including my happening, is that Happening, and that Happening is completely and unconditionally affirmed. All is well in the Great Mess.

From this perspective, there is nothing to do, nothing to attain, no conditions to meet—you are perfect in being whatever mess you presently are. Rejoice and be glad. Enjoy. For me, fully realizing no need for "enlightenment" would be enlightenment. Thankfulness arises.

But there is also the non-tautological side of being what we are—the psychological side in which we are in conflict with our actuality. We wish to be other than what we are. We are not being what we are. (I take "what we are" as our actual behavioral existence, not some phantom "true nature". "There is only this one moon; there is no second moon.") Although this psychological dissonance is also entirely affirmable, since it issues in self-discontent, we do well to address it. (Or am I only projecting? No matter; this is unavoidably about me, however much I speak of "us".)

We are considering three aspects of *de* here. There is ontological *de*—we cannot "stray from Dao" in that whatever we are and do is an expression of Dao. When we embrace and affirm our failure to appreciate this, that is *live* this, this is (discombobulated) *de*. And when we actually realize this first *de* in ourselves, this too is *de*.

The last two of these are conditional *de*—they can be realized or not. However, they both rest in an appreciation of their ultimate unconditionally.

We still want to know if this makes us "better", of course. God forbid that we should shirk our responsibility to be "good". But though Daoist *de* is not about being good, goodness follows nonetheless. The sage cares nothing for "good", which is precisely the cause of her being so.

IV

Speaking of the hypothetical sage, Zhuangzi has someone "recklessly" tell us: "While the mass of men are beleaguered and harried, the sage is dim and dense, standing shoulder to shoulder with the sun and moon, scooping up time and space and smooching them all together, leaving them all to their own slippery mush so that every enslavement is also an ennobling." (2:41)

Unpacking all this would require a full presentation of Zhuangzian philosophy. But this is not unusual; in the end, every facet of this philosophy implies all the rest. There seems to be a central idea, but in exploring it we discover that it is explained by other ideas that can likewise claim to be central. It's omnicentric—everything explains everything else. Every result is also the cause.

But we have to start somewhere, and in the context of this present series, I will focus on the final phrase: "Every enslavement is also an ennobling." This, in part, explains the value of discombobulated *de*.

Largely inspired by our addiction to right and wrong, our default motivation when confronted by something deemed unacceptable is to eradicate it. For Zhuangzi, however, it is only through the embrace of something so deemed that we are able to transcend it in soaring freedom. This too is the usefulness of the useless. Take away the problem and we lose the solution. Eradicate the resistance of the monsoonal wind and, like the mighty bird Peng, we could not take the highest flight of existence possible.

For Zhuangzi, it is not the transformation of the ceaselessly arising vicissitudes of life that is of first importance, but the transformation of our relationship to them. And this, not entirely surprisingly, often transforms the vicissitudes themselves.

Discombobulated *de*, I would suggest, is making skillful use of the mess that we are. The tidying up of that mess is secondary and consequential to this.

The sage takes the nature of the cosmos as her point of departure. She takes it as a "slippery mush"—not only is her own existence a messy business, but so too is that of the cosmos. It is ceaselessly transforming in a chaotic happening of formation and destruction. It is a Great Mess.

How are we any different?

The sage says "Yes, thank you" to the cosmic mess, and consequentially does the same with respect to the individual messes that she and we are. Our "every enslavement" is the means by which we can soar in the freedom of pan-affirmation.

V

Given the extent of my own mess, it is not surprising that I fully embrace discombobulated *de*. Or should I say *my* take on discombobulated *de*? It's curious how my interpretation of Zhuangzi so closely conforms to my own needs. Or is it that Zhuangzi's ambiguity invites a "build your own" kind of philosophizing?

This is probably the case, but there *is* an obvious bias for the misfit in Zhuangzi. And this is not coincidental; it bespeaks the overall flavor of his thinking which consistently goes against the grain of conventional values. In the passage quoted in the previous post we are told that the sage is "dim and dense". Is she really, or is she only seen as such?

Nor is this unique to Zhuangzi; it is a prominent theme within philosophical Daoism generally. Laozi pseudo-laments his own apparent misfittedness: "The masses have more than enough while I alone appear needy. I have the mind of a fool—so slow. Normal people are brilliant while I am dim. Normal people understand while I am dim-witted." (*Laozi* 20)

This is not simply obstinacy. In a world completely enthralled of yang and yang-ing, the advocate for yin can only seem out of step with the general march toward self-reification. This so permeates our ("modern") cultures that we hardly notice it anymore.

Own this and be a sexy somebody. Be seen as beautiful in this way. Be like "the world's most interesting man". Be rich and famous. Can't do that? Identify with those who are and let them live for you.

Today's "sages" hardly fit the perception of the sages that Daoism presents. Today's spiritual somebodies are seen as wise, charismatic, and powerful. Yang wins again. Beware the sages known to be.

But surely the true sage is not as she is perceived. She really *is* wise, charismatic and powerful, isn't she? Discombobulated *de* is only how she appears to the yang-ers. Perhaps this is all Zhuangzi had in mind—but I think otherwise. I think she *is* a mess, just like me. She just uses that mess to launch into the freedom of being who she is.

THE INDIFFERENCE OR
BIRDS
I – XI

(Please see the cover art for
"The Indifference of Birds")

I

For me, this drawing is a study of hope. It wonderfully illustrates the possibility of a hope of non-hope, that special freedom that obtains when our caring is not ruled by "benefit or harm" but rather fears no particular outcome. It is well worthy of meditating upon. The artist has entitled it "The Indifference of Birds".

I made the following observations to the artist:

I'm thinking of it as: Hope, Despair and the Indifference of Birds. Or: Hope comforts Despair while the birds don't care (or enjoy a day in the park).

I like the way Hope leans into and almost merges with Despair (our first focus) and then the birds turn us out and away.

His reply:

The form of the drawing is a triangle; the trinitarian nature of this doodlegadget is inescapable. A very pleasing riff, variation, and furthering—this is what it is to play where the object of the game is to keep the ball in motion, not to arrive at some final conclusion that would murder all the fun. The bubble-headed nature of dumb hopefulness, the uglification of a soul in despair, the grounded simplicity of gelassenheit*, all bound together in a three-cornered hat, a party hat not for saturday-night abandon but perfect for a stroll in the park wandering carefree.

95

*A Heideggarian neologism meaning "the spirit of *disponibilité* [availability] before What-Is which permits us simply to let things be in whatever may be their uncertainty and their mystery." (*Scott, Nathan A. (1969)*. *Negative Capability. Studies in the New Literature and the Religious Situation*. Quoted in Wikipedia).

Sounds incredibly Zhuangzian!

II

The couple is our first and primary focus. This is the human experience without external reference. He is in abject despair. She (or he—the figure seems a bit androgynous) comforts him. Which is the stronger figure? Despair. Despair is the fuller figure—starkly self-contained, unreachable. Hope is, as the artist tells us, "bubble-headed", and not even fully formed. Hope, for all her genuine and affirmable caring, is ultimately empty. What can she say? It will be alright. Will it? And if things turn for the better, won't they necessarily turn for the worse once again? All she can really provide are empty platitudes in the face of Unamuno's "tragic sense of life", namely that it has no sure purpose and must necessarily come to an ignoble end. "The god that shits" (Ernest Becker) loosens its bowls and takes its last.

I am reminded of Zhuangzi's assessment of the human condition: "When someone dies people say, 'He still lives in our hearts.' But in truth his body decayed and his mind went with it. This is our greatest sorrow. Isn't human experience completely bewildering?" (2:11) Hope in the end is but wishful thinking.

We are remarkable for our admirable resilience, nonetheless. It's amazing, really. This speaks to the power, the élan, of life itself. Hope dawns eternal, we say, even while knowing in our heart of hearts that it sets just as frequently and will eventually set forever. Every human hope is at root a false hope. Could there be a hope that is also a non-hope, one free of expectations and prescribed outcomes? Zhuangzi suggests there can.

III

This couple belongs together. They in fact give rise to each other. Despite being opposites, they seem to merge. Hope is there for Despair; Despair is there for Hope. They are co-dependent. Why is he in despair? Because he requires a hope that Hope cannot provide. Why does Hope offer hope? Because despair lurks in the heart of Hope as well.

We are pulled into this union of Hope and Despair. They are a couple. They are one. They are humanity solely in the context of a human perspective. They are one, even as opposites, but there is no resolution between them.

But here are two tiny birds looking in opposing directions, out and away. We might have missed or dismissed them but for the title, "The Indifference of Birds". This is somehow about them. Yet they care nothing for the main event, the drama unfolding beside them. They do not watch the couple, but out to nothing in particular. Nor do they together look up to a higher Reality, a solution, a resolution. That would involve them in the drama. Rather, they look out to indefinite and indifferent mystery.

IV

We have this huge human drama of Hope and Despair, but the title suggests we consider the tiny birds. They are looking out at nothing in particular because there is nothing in particular "out there" at which to look. They look in opposite directions because any direction will do. Every way we turn it is the same—Mystery.

The birds are tiny. They are dwarfed by the self-absorbed human drama that similarly absorbs us. We *are* human, after all. This is why the most obvious of realities, our grounding in nothing fixed and sure, is mostly forgotten; except deep in the heart of our subconscious anguish. The tiny birds represent the useless that Zhuangzi would have us understand as the most useful thing of all. They are the emptiness at the center of Laozi's wheel that makes the wheel useful. Daoism prioritizes Yin—non-existence, the empty, indefinite, unknowable, mystery—not because it trumps Yang—existence—but because existence wants to forget it. Yet without it we only see half the picture.

This would not be a problem except that it is. Hope and Despair are a couple, but we incorporate them both. And for all her admirable and affirmable ministrations Hope cannot console Despair. Despair is the realist, the honest one. If all were well in the human heart, half the picture or any fraction thereof would be just fine. But this is not the case, and thus a remedy would be helpful. But it cannot be a dishonest and inauthentic remedy—yet another hopeful platitude. It has to be grounded in our obvious groundlessness—our embedding in Mystery.

V

This is one picture and both the tiny birds and the human couple belong within it. They belong to the same world. In this, for all their differences, they are the same. Whether hoping, caring and despairing, or indifferent they are genuinely giving expression to their natures. This is their oneness. They are the same in being different. And just as we do not say of birds that they should care, so also we do not say of humans that they should be indifferent. Only in the case of humans there is an awareness of indifference, the apparent indifference of the universe as represented by two tiny birds. In this mutual embedding in Mystery there is also a oneness. This is our experience, our existential dangle, and as such must inform our living if we are to live authentically. The tiny birds have no such burden. In this we are "special".

This couple is doing what humans do. They care. They hope. And they despair. Hope arises naturally as the very élan of life. Life seeks to flourish in fullness. Let us then affirm and live this hope. But there is another hope, a hope of expectations, a hope that depends on certain outcomes, a hope uninformed by the indifference of Mystery. This hope generates despair and is in turn generated by despair. This is the hope that "adds to the process of life" and alienates us from our embedding in Mystery.

The hope that is non-hope is the hope that spontaneously arises from life itself; it requires no justification, for it depends on nothing. To live is to hope. Let us then live this hope. To live is to trust. Let us then live this trust.

VI

We have arrived at the central theme that I take away from this "doodle", though I do not presume that it was the artist's or that he had any intentional theme at all. I reflect upon what *happened* as I see it, not on intended meanings.

This theme is that there is a hope that is non-hope in the conventional sense, and it is only this hope that can truly energize us to fully engage in the life experience, both personal and social, without a subconscious enervating despair. The everyday hope of humanity is a hope *for* something. It has an object. And when that object is not realized hope is disappointed, and in things of great significance, this results in despair.

"Hope deferred makes the heart sick, but when the desire comes it is the tree of life" (Proverbs 13:12). The Bible got it at least half right. But then the Bible is all about false hopes. False hope is that which generates it's opposite, despair. (Just as belief generates doubt.) And why do we hope? Because we are in despair.

This simultaneous generation of opposites is used by Zhuangzi to suggest another, higher perspective that both transcends and embraces them. Can we both hope and despair while remaining ever hopeful? If we can, then we will have a kind of non-hope that laughs at and wanders in both hope and despair even as we experience them—and we most certainly will.

There is logic in this. Opposites not only generate each other, they also cancel out each other. Hope is already despair and despair is already hope. Is there really then either hope or despair? If not, can we not then unite them to form a oneness, a hope of non-hope that depends on nothing?

But why a hope that is non-hope and not a despair that is non-despair? Because though they are the same, hope connotes the affirmation of life, and life is that affirming.

It is not desire fulfilled that is "the tree of life", but hope—ceaseless, non-contingent affirmation. Life is hope. Hope is the fruit of the tree of life, a tree rooted in Mystery and thus no purveyor of false hopes.

VII

The hope that is non-hope is that hope that is an unmediated expression of life itself. And though we have followed Zhuangzi in making a logical argument for how we can understand the dynamics of the simultaneous generation of the opposites hope and despair and thereby unite and transcend them, we must also now follow him in his appeal for a pre- and post-cognitive re-integration with the life experience itself. The reasoning mind is a wonderful thing and we make the best use of it when we discover its limits and continue on to where it cannot go.

This is where we become mystics. This is where we "let our mind spring to life from its rootedness in the unthinking parts of ourselves" (23; p 99). Our mysticism, in this instance, is inward, a re-integration with our mysterious selves. We let ourselves happen. We become that happening. And we let the hope and trust that is that happening flourish without mediation as an expression of what it is for us to be.

This is the heart of spontaneity. Daoist spontaneity is the experience of allowing ourselves to happen without the mediation of the cognitive mind. Thus our hope neither has nor requires a reason to be. It simply is. Rooted in Mystery, it depends on nothing in particular.

All things are self-so, spontaneously and mysteriously arising. Even our dysfunctionality is spontaneously so. Even our non-spontaneity is spontaneously so. We affirm it all. Yet the very facility that enables our dysfunction, our bondage to cognition and its many discriminations, similarly allows a spontaneity that is spontaneously so. This is to harmonize with life as it most essentially is.

VIII

In such a simple tableau it would be remiss to overlook any of its subjects. I have yet to mention the tree above and the paving stones below. I have taken them, together with the bench, as suggesting a city park. Their indifference, however, is as ever much in evidence as that of the birds; perhaps more so in that we expect it of them even more than of more sentient beings. So let us also bring them into our unifying embrace. Let us find that sense in which all these elements, including this couple, are the same and unite them to form a oneness. But we, too, are this couple—can we see ourselves in this one tableau of indifference and harmonize with it?

When the carpenter Shi dismissed the worthiness of an immense tree because it was useless to his purposes, the tree appeared to him in a dream and said, "Who are you, a mere man about to die, to judge me (who have lived for many hundreds of years)? Are we not in any case both members of the same class, namely beings?" (4:18) In realizing this both Shi and we will experience the non-contingent worthiness of all things, not to the diminishing of our own, but rather to its unfathomable increase.

The proto-Daoist Shen Dao exhorted, "Realize the indifference of an insentient thing. A clump of earth never strays from the Dao." His detractors said this was a dao for the dead, not the living, but they had yet to realize how life and death form a single body. These paving stones shout this liberating message the loudest of all, if only we have ears to hear.

What is of Nature and what is of Humanity? This park bench is both. It invites us to understand human artifice in its equivalence to that of a hive of bees. We cannot stray from Dao, even as we naturally do.

We are ever invited to realize a higher view, and in that "bask everything in the broad daylight of Heaven."

IX

In this second to last post in this series we would do well to return to the artist's own description of this "doodle". (This can be found in I.) There he says, *"this is what it is to play where the object of the game is to keep the ball in motion, not to arrive at some final conclusion that would murder all the fun."* The tiny birds look out and away, speaking not only of their indifference, but also to the indefiniteness of their focus. Things always remain open and inconclusive; that is how it is that we can play at all. They could be looking anywhere, for everywhere is the same Mystery.

Yet in saying so, and in having interpreted every element within the tableau, we must admit to having "murdered all the fun". This is perfectly acceptable, and possibly even necessary, but now we must make murdering the fun part of the fun. We must self-efface our formulaic pronouncements, our "final conclusions", and put the ball back into play. We must return the doodle to its own mystery, and let the reader have her or his own fun playing within it.

Like Zhuangzi's "spill-over-goblet words" where the words tip, self-empty and are forgotten when their intent is realized, here too we acknowledge our formulae as the myths that they are. Yet where every pronouncement is necessarily myth, our myths are not without their virtues. Only their greatest virtue resides in their self-awareness as myths. In the land of the blind, the one-eyed man is king. We can all open that one eye in the acknowledgement of the "obvious", that we all live together in the land of not-knowing.

X

I conclude this series with a word of appreciation for the artist who made his art available while choosing to remain anonymous. This appreciation could not be better expressed than by speaking of the beauty of his art. It has moved me profoundly, and I can think of no greater praise than that.

There is so much than can be said of this "doodle"—its compositional and meaningful integrity, the subtleties in the presentation of its components, and so much more that is well beyond my reach. However, I will focus on just one small thing— something that I learned from my own brief excursion into doodling. And this is the unspeakable beauty of an honest line (which, alas, I seldom realized). One single line can be a consummate artistic expression.

An honest line is one that happens. It shows no hesitation. It happens as the spontaneous expression of a deeply cultivated dao. It is the circle made without compasses; the straight line made without a straight-edge. It is the dismembering of an ox as if performing a sacred dance.

Though this work is doubtless full of such lines, the ones that leave me in awe here are those that form the bubble-head of Hope. They are not drawn; they happen. To them I could burn incense. Words cannot reach them.

If art is a message, then let us say together with King Hui, "From my lowly cook, I have learned how to nourish life!" The cultivated spontaneity of art is emblematic of the possibility of cultivating the spontaneity of life.

PUNISHED BY HEAVEN
I – VI

I

Though he makes fast and free with Confucius as a character, one still senses that Zhuangzi respects the historical figure. This is not the case with many of his representations in other, later chapters of the *Zhuangzi*, where he is held up to ridicule and diminished. This comes with the rise of a more sectarian form of Daoism and the competition for political influence. This needn't surprise us given the near universal abandonment of the spirit of original insight in favor of the default human inclination for yang-ing. It is the co-option of transcendent experience by religious-mindedness.

Mostly, Zhuangzi uses Confucius as a spokesman for his own philosophy, though that is clearly quite contrary to Confucianism. This creates a sense of irony, a logical disconnect between "fact" and words that casts the entire project—and every such project—into ambiguity and doubt. And that's good.

There is playfulness here; and playfulness requires an underlying lack of seriousness. Yes, Zhuangzi believes his point of view works best, but since that point of view affirms all points of view, heaven and earth will not topple if his does not win out over others. The real point is to be able to play and then to play. Zhuangzi is at play.

There are times, however, when Confucius is used as the fall-guy—the guy who just can't do it. There is irony here too because he does actually *get* it; he can appreciatively articulate Zhuangzi's philosophy as well as Zhuangzi himself—he just can't live it. He is "punished by Heaven".

And that's okay. It's great to be runner-up, also ran, or even scratched. It's all good. All that we would hope for is that we made the best use of our natural abilities. And even failing of that can be wandered in. If all things cannot be wandered in, then nothing can; for wandering is depending on nothing. We can even wander in our inability to wander.

We can only wander when there's something to wander in. Being punished by Heaven works as well as anything else.

II

Two passages in the Inner Chapters speak to this theme of being "punished by Heaven". The one in which the term is used explicitly has it assigned to Confucius by another. (5:13) The other has Confucius himself admitting to his inability to follow the Zhuangzian dao though he deems it best—he declares himself "a victim of Heaven". (6:47)

What these two passages have in common is an understanding that the transformative experience that the Zhuangzian dao advocates is not possible for everyone. Indeed, we might also wonder if it's possible for *any*one—given that only fictional characters are represented as having achieved it. This is profoundly significant, needless to say. There are ramifications aplenty.

Ironically, there is something truly liberating here. We're off the hook! We can step off the treadmill! Nature itself has disallowed our so-called spiritual attainment! Now we can just get on with enjoying being who and what we are! We can shout Yes! to "me"!

But wait—if awareness of our not being able to attain liberation is liberating, then aren't we being liberated just the same? We are. Or at least we can be. We can be even when we can't be. Indeed, we can be *because* we can't be. "*Every* enslavement is also an ennobling." (2:41)

Still, there's still some conditionality implied here. An *awareness* of our victimhood is necessary. And how do we discover that? By trying to attain liberation. We must try in order to fail. And when we've failed, we can continue trying just the same, albeit now as informed by a lack of a realizable goal.

But if this is how it is, then it is really not the goal that counts at all but only the process. What counts is *living*. Now. Just as we are. With nothing to become in order to be deemed "acceptable".

Now *that's* liberating!

III

Toeless Shushan, whose foot had been amputated for some crime, went to Confucius for spiritual instruction. But Confucius rejected him because of his past failing. Yet Toeless turned the tables and rebuked Confucius for his failure to realize the equalization in non-discrimination that is Dao: "Heaven covers all things. Earth supports all things. I used to think, Sir, that you were just like Heaven and earth—". (5:13)

This is not unlike the purported words of Jesus: God "makes his sun to rise on the evil and on the good, and sends rain on the just and on the unjust." (Matthew 5:45) The implication? Be God-like in your tolerance and equanimity. Most Christians also appear to be punished by Heaven in this regard—not unlike the rest of us.

Daoism, needless to say, believes in no God, but the principle is the same. Nor does being punished by Heaven imply volition or karmic consequence—if we take Heaven to be Nature, then it is just the facts of life. If I want to flap my arms and fly, I will discover I am punished by Heaven in this regard. It's not in my nature.

Toeless understood that it was not in Confucius's nature to be able "to fly without wings", to experience Zhuangzian soaring. When he consulted with Laozi, however, this sage suggested an imaginative remedy: "Why don't you simply let him see life and death as a single string, acceptable and unacceptable as a single thread, thus releasing him from his fetters?"

But Toeless replied: "Heaven itself has inflicted this punishment on him—how can he be released?"

117

Confucius was stung and confessed his own failing in this regard. Would he then be able to make use of *this* and soaringly equalize acceptable and unacceptable? Probably not. He likely carried on with the burden of his own sense of failing and self-judgment which, of course, only gave further impetus to his projection of judgment upon others.

But hey, let's see if we can't let our sun rise on him as well.

IV

Confucius' declaration of his own inability to be free of his bondage to conventional values is especially enlightening. Having been sent to represent him at a (presumably) Daoist wake, a disciple returns scandalized that the mourning friends were singing silly songs and generally making merry. (6:45-7) But Confucius explains that these are those "who roam outside the lines" of convention. He, on the other hand, must "roam inside the lines". He then goes on to extol the virtues and benefits of what he admittedly does not practice.

Since he apparently would rather be free to roam outside the lines, the disciple asks why he does not do so. "As for myself," Confucius replies, "I am a victim of Heaven. But that is something that you and I might share." It is something we all likely share.

We might first take this to imply the "superiority" of the Zhuangzian dao to the Confucian dao, and this is certainly part of the equation. Zhuangzi thinks his dao makes for a happier life. But if we actually apply that dao, that is, adopt its perspective, then there can be no such thing as inferior or superior. They are equalized "under the broad daylight of Heaven".

The ability to hold these two apparently contradictory views simultaneously is walking two roads.

This paradoxical relationship also obtains between the ideal and the actual and permeates the entirety of any project of self-cultivation we might pursue. We are running a race already won. Why do we not then just kickback and "do lots of nothing in our homeland of not even anything"? Because we too are victims of Heaven, and as such have a race we cannot help but run.

"Self-cultivation" implies a perceived need. And even when we understand that ideally there is no need for self-cultivation, it is only self-cultivation that can make that proximally actual. This dialectic does not reduce to logic—no more than life does.

V

We are often told by advocates of New Age philosophies that it's our "birthright" to realize whatever "spiritual" enlightenment they imagine. This usually comes with promises of discovering our "true nature" and "true purpose". Even were we to believe in such essentially religious concepts, the idea of being a "victim of Nature" puts the nix on the assertion of any "birthright". It tells us that this is equivalent to declaring that we can all be virtuoso violinists—even though some of us might have been born armless.

Does any of this really matter? From the point of view of Zhuangzian Daoism it ultimately matters not at all. No purposive trajectory is believed to be written in the heavens. No salvation is required for individual things or for the Cosmos. All resolves to wellness—where wellness is whatever it resolves to. No change is necessary where change is all there is. Whatever we do or believe is of no eternal consequence.

Is this position also essentially religious? It can be; but it need not be if we can remember that it is only an imaginative interpretation of the world where some such interpretation is unavoidable.

Still, does any of this at least matter *practically*? I usually make the case that it does—an armless aspirant to violin virtuosity is less likely to be at peace with the givens of her or his existence. In the end, however, this can only be an individual and subjective determination. Where it's all messy in any case, there's little room for judging between messes.

In terms of universal applicability, the bottom seems to have dropped out of this present project. Indeed, its only relevance is to my own mess.

VI

I have suggested that the realization of one's "victimhood" vis-à-vis the ability to realize Zhuangzian soaring can itself be an occasion for soaring. It could not be otherwise where soaring implies depending on nothing in particular—not even soaring.

This also implies the value of soaring. And that implies a perceived need. And that is a kind of dependence. We are caught in a conundrum of our own making. What are we to do? Live the mess and its contradictions, is the best I can answer.

As presented here, this soaring seems to be an optional activity—it is something that we choose to do. There is also a sense in which we can do nothing but. Guo Xiang made much of this. Commenting on the contrast between the vastness of the mighty bird Peng and the tiny birds that scoff at him (Chapter One), he writes:

"Though some are larger and some are smaller, every being without exception is released into the range of its own spontaneous attainments, so that each being relies on its own innate character, each deed exactly matching its own capabilities. Since each fits perfectly into precisely the position it occupies, all are equally far-reaching and unfettered [descriptive adjectives of Zhuangzi's soaring]." (p 129)

This likely inspired my mantra: I am perfect by virtue of my being perfectly who I am. This is the "all is well" that pertains to every individual thing just as it is. Soaring, in this case, is simply being who we are—victimized or not. We all soar.

IMAGINATIVE
MEDITATION
I – V

I

It may well be that Zhuangzi made use of the meditative techniques of his peers; surely, he must have at least dabbled in them? Graham has him previously being a disciple of Huizi (a Logician) and before that of Yang Chu (the so-called hedonist—self first!), so perhaps he *was* a bit of a dabbler. Aren't we all?

Taken as a whole, however, I think the Inner Chapters settle on a less conventional technique for self-cultivation: imaginative meditation.

I take complete non-dependence as an essential attribute of Zhuangzi's "wandering"; and yet he only introduces it as a hypothetical: "But suppose you depended on nothing ..?" (1:8; paraphrased) Why should this surprise us given that this dependence or non-dependence is entirely a matter of psychological orientation? We're not talking about Reality here.

The idea of imagination being a gateway to a transformation in consciousness doesn't sit well with the truth-seeking mind. But Zhuangzi has reconciled himself with his inability to find the Truth. (An advantage of having extensively dabbled?) How then could he represent transformation as somehow a consequence of truth-finding?

At first blush, Buddhism might have no problem with imaginative meditation; it can easily be taken as an *upaya*, a skillful means, to the discovery of Truth. Conventional truth, which is to say not-the-real truth, is the only way by which to arrive at the real Truth. Like a raft, when it's gotten you to the other side of the river, you let it go.

SCOTT P. BRADLEY

But this is not Zhuangzi's position. He imagines no such ultimate Truth. He remains in the world of "Drift and Doubt". He depends on no Truth. He wanders on this side of the river.

Having said that, he *does* imagine truth... lots of them, whichever one works. The difference is that he is aware that it is and must remain only an imaginative exercise. It too is a skillful means, albeit one without any idealist pretense.

II

Imagine our every interpretation of ourselves and the apparent world as a kind of dreaming. This is quite different than saying it *is* a dream—how could we know that? But the very fact that we don't know it suggests that whatever interpretative view we *do* decide on is equivalent to a dreaming. This is Zhuangzi's point of view. (2:41-3)

So, here we are in an epistemological state of dreaming. What are we to do? First, we have to acknowledge that such is the case. But we typically do not recognize that this is a dreaming at all—we take our point of view as correct and true—things are actually as we see them. We interpret the dream within the dream, and that's the end of it.

Is this a problem? What problems ultimately endure? Within Zhuangzi's dream, all things are equalized, all ends up well, and therefore, even the present problems are informed of wellness. This has its present psychological and sociological advantages. And this is the only real justification for deciding on this dream.

The alternative dream, namely that problems have enduring, eternal consequences, creates its own problems. This view, it seems to me, is nonsensical unless we also believe that we, as fixed identities, also eternally endure. We need to endure so as to take our problems with us. And if we do this, then our present problems, our moral failings, are of momentous importance.

I know of no major religion that does not posit a hell, at least in the popular imagination. There needs to be an eternal repository for the unresolved problems and moral failings of our present. Only this can give right and wrong the immovable foundation that they require. There needs to be consequences.

I will leave it to the reader to consider the negative psychological and sociological impacts of such a dream.

Thus imaginative meditation is really not so different than our everyday dreaming. It's just that we make conscious choices about what to dream. We choose those interpretations of the unknowable that bring us the outcomes most conducive to our individual and collective flourishing.

All that is required is that we give up Truth.

III

Zhuangzi's entire philosophy is essentially an imaginative exercise; after his critique of reason and his rejection of taking our minds as our teacher, he had very little choice but to go in this direction.

There is also that side of his philosophy that suggests we live in a manner altogether unmediated by thought. This is Daoist spontaneity. "Let your mind spring forth from its rootedness in the unthinking parts of yourself," suggests one of his interpreters. (23; p 99) The most immediate question then is how do we manage this?

When Yan practiced "fasting of the heart/mind" he discovered that it is really a kind of inner emptiness that "moves" him. (4:10) The suggestion is that we also be aware that we are so moved—moved by our empty self, not by the self that thinks itself "full and real" and thus thinks it needs to mediate its living. Spontaneity is letting the happening happen.

Fasting of the heart/mind seems to be a form of meditation that Zhuangzi himself likely sometimes practiced. But what is lacking in his writing generally is a clear advocacy for this as the be all and end all of his suggested methodology. We know from those who do advocate this one method, both then and now, that they can hardly speak of anything else.

Much more frequently advocated in his writing is a kind of imaginative mediation. This is my interpretive take; he makes no such explicit statement. This is in keeping with the general ambiguity of his writing as a whole, and it is that ambiguity that makes possible imaginative exercises in the first place.

The use of one's imagination is a use of one's mind. We need not stop thinking, but only to stop thinking that thinking is living or that thinking can discover fixed and sure formulae by which to live. Taking one's mind as one's teacher refers to these.

Imaginative meditation is thus quite different than most forms of meditation where one attempts to stop thinking altogether. It is not a rejection of that method, but only a possibly complementary alternative. It is the use of one's mind to transform the ultimately unavoidable use of one's mind. A point of view is unavoidable, and the point of this exercise is to enable that point of view to be as beneficial as possible.

IV

A disgraced man named Wang Tai whose foot has been amputated as punishment for some crime has more disciples than Confucius, and a disciple of Confucius wants to know how this could be. (5:2ff) Unlike Confucius, he teaches nothing, yet people come to him empty and leave full. He practices "a wordless instruction, a formless way of bringing the mind to completion". Confucius admits that he too should be his disciple, but something has held him back.

Confucius' disciple further enquires: "How exactly does he make use of his mind?" This is a remarkably different line of inquiry in Zhuangzi's exploration of sagacity. Making use of one's mind to bring the mind to completion—isn't this precisely what we are supposed to eschew?

The relevance of this use of the mind to the method of imaginative meditation should be clear; for that is exactly what it is.

Confucius answers with a powerful imaginative exercise of his own: Looked at from the point of view of their differences, all things are unique. "But looked at from the point of view of their sameness, all things are one... You just release the mind to play in the harmony of all *de*. Seeing what is one and the same to all things, nothing is ever felt to be lost."

The mind is thus used *playfully*—imaginatively. And this is its "completion". "Hence when the understanding consciousness comes to rest in what it does not know, it has reached its utmost." (2:36) But that's not the end of it; the mind does not disappear, but goes on to have fun. Released from the need to know, it can now wander among all possibilities.

Confucius' disciple summarizes: "He uses his mind to discover [the capacities of] his mind and then makes use of that mind of his to develop a mind for the constant."

"Constant" translates *chang*. What is this constant? *That* is a matter of interpretive bias. Curiously, *chang* can be translated "eternal", and this mind can become the Eternal Mind. This works well for those of essentialist leanings. But Ziporyn suggests that it rather refers to a mind made "sustainable" in its identification with the imagined oneness of all things wherein "nothing is ever felt to be lost. (p 33; note 6)

The consequence of this for Wang Tai is that the loss of his foot is of no more importance than a clump of soil tossed away. "He takes all that his consciousness knows and unifies it into a singularity, so that his mind has never once died." He is fearless because he has nothing to lose when identified with that in which nothing can be lost.

V

Imagine psychologically depending on absolutely nothing. All that happens or could happen would then be acceptable. The totality of experience would be affirmable. All would be well in the imagined Cosmos.

Imagine so identifying with change that no change could threaten you.

Imagine taking life and death as a single string, one body. Your death would then be as affirmable as your life.

Imagine the oneness of all things in their sameness. All things would then be as precious as you are.

These are all imaginative exercises. None of them are demonstrably true. But then no interpretive point of view is. They are simply choices about how to respond to the life experience. Other responses are possible; other responses are equally justifiable; which one best enables you to live as happily as you can manage?

SCOTT P. BRADLEY

CIRCUMSTANCE AND OPPORTUNITY
I – XIII

I

I'm re-reading Steve Coutinho's *An Introduction to Daoist Philosophies*, which I highly recommend. So many "introductions" start off with wrong-footed presuppositions that one that does not is refreshingly helpful even if necessarily cursory.

The word *ming* is typically translated as "fate" or "destiny", both of which can be taken to imply something quite different from Zhuangzi's meaning. Coutinho suggests "circumstance", a more neutral term that avoids the ill-fitting connotations of the former two.

"Circumstance" is a concept of critical importance to Zhuangzian "Daoism". It speaks to the "unavoidable" that surrounds and permeates our every existential moment. This constitutes our interface with the world as we experience it, and is thus relational. Circumstance is more than simply the objective conditions of life; it is also the manner in which we interact with them. This being the case, every circumstance is an *opportunity* to nurture our experience of life—to further realize its potential flourishing.

Coutinho quotes Zhuangzi in this regard: "To tend to your heart-mind so that sadness and joy do not sway or move it; to understand what you can do nothing about and to rest content in it as Circumstance, this is the height of potency" (Watson, p 60).

In this series I hope to explore this pivotal *activity* in some depth. We might start by seeing that it is in fact an activity. It is work. Ideally, it would be no such thing in having been fully accomplished, but we are not sages and thus have work to do. This is self-cultivation.

Though it can seem tediously repetitive, always it seems necessary to also step back off the narrow road of human self-involvement and onto the road of a more cosmic perspective. Self-cultivation is best accomplished in the light of its being ultimately unnecessary. This is likely a condition for *wuwei*, doing non-doing. We are perfect by virtue of our being perfectly who we are, just as we are—an absolutely unavoidable cosmic circumstance. There are no conditions we are required to meet. All is well. Now that we have realized that we are perfect, we can get to work on getting "better".

II

Translating *ming* as "circumstance" rather than as the more common "fate", or even "destiny", has the advantage of avoiding two misunderstandings which are decidedly not part of the Daoist worldview—purpose and fatalism. From the point of view of Daoism, nothing happens for a *reason*. Nor did anything that *has* happened *have to* happen.

Neither of these negations is intended as a definitive assertion of the contrary, but simply returns us to the real experience of our existential not-knowing. Perhaps there *is* a divine plan, and maybe everything *is* pre-determined. Who knows? The point is to authentically live in harmony with our actual experience.

The hunger for things to have a *purpose* is one of our strongest yearnings. Why are we here? Or vastly more importantly, why am *I* here? For this reason, religiously-minded formulae typically promise to reveal our "true purpose". This serves to reify us as forever a someone completely integrated into a cosmic Plan. What could be better? Since we clearly need comforting, why would we want to disabuse those of what comfort they find here? Would we snatch a teddy bear from a child because it is not "real"?

But let me be honest and admit that this present project is in many respects my own teddy bear. For this reason I call my blabberings a philosophy of cope. In my defense, I would point out that it is *awareness* of the fact that makes all the difference. The trajectory toward authenticity (sagacity) is in any case, as I repeatedly aver, an open-ended and messy business.

Since our yearning for purpose is so strong we might ask if it is not therefore "innate". By Daoist reckoning, if it's innate, it is to be affirmed and nurtured. I make the case for flourishing as the highest good, because it is innate to life. Life *is* the élan of self-flourishing. It needs no justification. Can we say the same for the yearning for purpose? This is an important question because it helps illuminate the frontlines of Zhuangzi's fight for greater authenticity against those inclinations that contribute to the contrary. I will leave this issue for the next post.

III

There is an argument for the existence of "God" that states that since we want "him" to exist, "he" must. Why else would we have been created thus? This reasoning is too specious and question-begging to require serious consideration. It presupposes what it "proves". I mention it here only because it parallels the belief that, since we yearn for an ultimate purpose for ourselves and (consequentially) the cosmos, there must be such a purpose.

Zhuangzi's admonition that we not "take our minds as our teacher" establishes what he sees as the frontline of the battle between authenticity and inauthenticity. Because we want to "understand" ourselves and the world does not mean that we can. We can certainly understand much *about* these, but we can never draw the sack closed; we can never reach the end that alone can justify the beginnings. What is the alternative? Living. Because we do in fact have minds that are intrinsically dualistic as evinced in our belief that we *have* a life (rather than that we *are* a life), the movement back to more spontaneous living is a *mystical* leap (where mystical simply means moving beyond the reasoning mind). I call this surrender in trust. Zhuangzi, more objectively, calls it "adding nothing to the process of life". Thankfulness and unmediated joy arise from being the life that we are.

The yearning for an ultimate purpose, I would suggest, is a function of the reasoning mind and should likewise not be taken as our teacher. Life is its own "purpose", and that has no obvious connection to a logically required ultimate purpose.

In many respects, Zhuangzi resembles a cold-blooded empiricist. Just the facts, ma'am. He is no airy-fairy romanticist or religionist. He arrives at his "free and carefree wandering" through *yiming*, "making use of the light". Ziporyn (self-admittedly "controversially") translates "the Illumination of the Obvious". His approach is phenomenological. He asks, How is life experienced, not, How can life be made to make sense?

This "battle" between authentic and inauthentic living needs, of course, to be understood in the light of a broader perspective that appreciates that sense in which they are both affirmable. The "petty-minded" dove and the vast-minded Peng are both simply living out their natures. Our yearning for purpose is how we typically manifest, and although there is a better (happier) alternative, the more authentic view does not completely negate the lesser. Somewhere in here is the power to choose, but we are in no position to draw the lines too firmly. Living the lesser in the light of the higher is, in any case, perhaps the best we can do.

IV

We are considering how philosophical Daoism takes *ming* (unavoidable circumstance) as a ubiquitous opportunity for self-cultivation. We can only choose how to respond to it; we can never escape it. It is in every way the essential condition of our existence. Have we chosen to be born? No? Then everything that follows thereafter is *ming*.

If "people take to Dao as fish take to water", then Dao is not the conditional medium *through* which we move, but *how* we move through it. It is not the medium—something distinct from our psychological involvement—but our interface with it. [The author of this quote probably thought otherwise.] *We create dao*. Every dao—and there are as many as there are pairs of feet to walk them—is the creative interface of our actively being in a world.

Zhuangzi's dao is Dao as the confluence of all daos. It's just another dao, albeit an all-inclusive dao. A most paradoxical dao. Metaphysical Dao there might be, but its only presence is by way of its absence. This is the most fundamental ontological *ming*—the condition of our inescapable adriftedness.

Circumstance (*ming*) is not a thing. If we translate "fate", we might envision some *purposive force* external to circumstance, but circumstance is, just as its etymology suggests, "all-around standing" alone. The concluding vignette of the "The Great Source as Teacher" chapter (6) of the *Zhuangzi* has a man lamenting that he can find no ultimate cause for the physical extremity in which he finds himself. There is none discernable. He calls this *ming*. Mencius, Zhuangzi's contemporary, recognizes the same: *Ming* is "what arrives although nothing makes it arrive" (*Mencius* 5A7). ["Dao does nothing, though nothing is left undone."] The inexplicability of *ming* is also *ming*.

Fang Yizhi (1611-1671) comments on this passage (6:57): "This is a man standing right at the mouth of the great furnace" (p 205). This is where we are transformed—not just through our awareness of *ming*, but also in the disquiet an anguish it causes in us. "Would you say that 'a white horse crying in pain under the glow of the clouds' is anything other than the Great Source as Teacher? If so, however much you spin your abstruse theories, you are still separated by an ever so thin layer from the real heaven and the real earth. You have not yet perceived that in the Dao there is only this one moon; there is no second moon."

V

Ming (circumstance) is what has *happened* and is now *happening*. Is there anything that "exists" that hasn't happened? Is there anything that is not presently continuing to happen? The Universe and all it contains has happened and continues to happen. I like to call the cosmos—whatever that is—the Great Happening. If we can imagine every happening as absolutely inseparable from that Happening—*as* that Happening—, then we will get a sense of what Zhuangzi is after when he says, "hand it all over to the unavoidable (*ming*) ". He identifies the cosmos with Transformation (*hua*) and suggests that we identify with that. Identify with ceaseless change and what changes can disturb you?

I call this *movement* of identification "surrender in trust". It is a surrender because it finds resistance in us. We naturally want to hold onto a fixed-identity that assures our eternal continuity. Since this seems ridiculous on the face of it, we are caught in a bind of clinging to what must almost certainly be lost. We fear the loss of ourselves. We fear death. Identified with Everything, there is nowhere for anything to get lost. This is "hiding the world in the world".

This movement also involves *trust*. It is not resignation. It is an act of complete unconditional affirmation. It is saying, Yes, thank you! for Everything. Trust is not belief. There is nothing to believe. It could be said that we believe that all is well, but trust is what life is. Trust is a spontaneous expression of life. Our every waking moment is permeated by trust. Real trust is not mediated by belief.

Is this then the Truth of things? Not at all. This is just an *imagined* point of view. If we understand that *whatever* life-view we hold is an imagined point of view, then we are free to choose the one that makes for our greatest enjoyment of life. This is the point for Zhuangzi's critique of logic and reason—to "release our minds to play".

Every circumstance, which is to say every possible happening, is an opportunity for surrender in trust, and every such movement is transformative. How so? Let's not get all metaphysically fuzzy— let's just say that it provides a moment of thankfulness and joy. And who knows, maybe that will become a habit.

VI

There are many genera of circumstance, ranging from what seems necessarily unavoidable in every case to what was avoidable only a moment ago, but is now unavoidable. Examples of this latter might be: the consequences of having just jumped off a bridge, having made a wrong turn, or being rear-ended by a drunk driver. *Choice* has played a role in each, but each is nonetheless now an immediately unavoidable circumstance. We will explore the opportunities presented by this genus anon; in this post we will begin to consider the necessarily unavoidable.

"Life and death are both very serious matters", Zhuangzi has Confucius say, "but they do not bother [the sage]" (5:2). These are the two great unavoidables of the human experience. It might be argued that they too were at some point avoidable—one's life is a consequence of the decisions of one's parents, and death would be avoidable were it not for one's life—but in being alive one now faces death (and aging) as the profoundest unavoidable circumstance.

Life and death are what concern Zhuangzi most. The idea that it could be otherwise makes us smile. Nevertheless, many philosophers immerse themselves in all manner of arcane studies, or even very important ones (political theory, language theory, etc.), that do not in fact address these fundamentals of our existence. Some fault Zhuangzi for his lack of political theory (and consequently assign him one by default), but a moment's reflection illuminates how, if one begins with the most immediate experience of our existence, everything else becomes derivative.

The consideration of life and death necessarily involves a movement from the objective and social to the specific and individual. Zhuangzi has been identified as a pioneer in making this shift. Once we have followed him there, we wonder that we would have wanted to begin anywhere else. Doing otherwise seems more like an act of avoidance than one of "getting on with life".

Taking one's actual individual subjective experience as one's point of departure need not end in individualism. Neither the extreme of collectivism, where the individual is a mere cog in the machine—a cipher, nor individualism, where one is oblivious of others or one's connectedness to others, genuinely represents the human experience. The most authentic inquiry into the human experience, however, must begin with that most immediate experience itself, and that is unavoidably a *personal* individual experience.

VII

Death is one of Zhuangzi's favorite subjects. This seems reasonable when we consider that his entire project was about life—specifically, how to get the most possible enjoyment out of it. Death, the apparent negation of life, does tend to cast a certain pall over life, as I think we can all agree. It behooves us, therefore, to understand life in the context of death.

Death is circumstance—the greatest unavoidable event facing us all (and taking away those we love in the meantime). Death is therefore also opportunity. Life is a "school of hard knocks" whatever cultural or economic privilege we might enjoy. "Knocks" are our teachers. Death is the grand-daddy of all "knocks" and thus an especially important teacher.

This school is also a "school of cope". Zhuangzi has his methods for dealing with death, but we should not think that these, or any other attempt to put the fear of death (aging and dying) to rest, can be final, definitive and completely successful. We must also be our fear—not deny it, but live it. There is freedom in this, too. Transcendence and transformation are more relational, psychological, than "actual".

My death is good. For those inclined to mantras, Zhuangzi would suggest you give this one a go. Meditation on this with a view to actually experiencing it is yet another "gate" into Zhuangzi's vision of free and carefree wandering.

Zhuangzi suggests we imagine life and death as a single body—one united reality. Such an imaginative movement also opens up into unity with the cosmos. We "hide the world in the world", realize a cosmic identification, when we unite with death. Death is the great out-there.

"Because I think my life good, so also do I think my death good", says Zhuangzi. Having united life and death, the perceived goodness of life carries over into death. Life and death are inseparable. If my life is good, so also must be my death. (If this is not how we already think, then this imaginative exercise can open us up to new possibilities.)

The goodness of death is not in contrast to the miseries of life, but a consequence of the goodness of life. This is the greatest possible affirmation. What an opportunity! It is not morbidity, but jubilant affirmation. Yes! Thankfulness! It's all good!

These are all just words. But there is something else here; something visceral; something transformative. The only way beyond mere words is to actually viscerally engage with their intent to the extent of experiencing them. This is imaginative meditation. My death is good. Experience understanding.

VII

My death is good. If my death is good, then the whole cosmic ball of wax is also good. (We know, of course, that the cosmos in not a ball of wax since there'd have to be something that was not this ball; but since this applies to whatever we say of it, this one works as well as any other.) All is Well.

Why is All Well? Because we say it is. Why do we say it is? Because, having surrendered ourselves in affirming trust into the Totality, we have harmonized our sense of the goodness of life with its larger context.

Why do we ask why? Because we believe there needs to be an objective *reason* that justifies saying so. What's the proof? There is none.

"If my life is good, so also is my death good". Why is my life good? Because I love and value it as such. But why? Because this is what life is and does. Life is an ever-affirming élan. Why would we want to question life? This is taking our mind as our teacher. This is throwing the proverbial spanner into the process of life. This is ruining good sex by ruminating on the why of it.

Why is my death good? Because my life is good, and life and death form one body. Without death there is no life. Without life there is no death. When these "are no longer coupled as opposites, that is called Dao as Convergence, the convergence of all daos" (2:17; emended). The unity of life and death is Dao. You want to "find" Dao? Let your mind be Dao-ed.

"Hence, all things are neither formed nor destroyed, for these two also open into each other, connecting to form a oneness. It is only someone who really gets all the way through them that can see how the two sides open into each other to form a oneness" (2:22).

Absolutely everything perceived, whether tangible or intangible, imagined or real, is a circumstance, and every circumstance is an opportunity to experience a bit of Dao. Absolutely everything is a "gate" into transcendence. Some gates loom larger than others, however; and among these, death looms largest of all. What an opportunity!

IX

"To tend to your heart-mind so that sadness and joy do not sway or move it; to understand what you can do nothing about and to rest content in it as Circumstance, this is the height of potency" (*Zhuangzi*, 4; Watson, p 60).

What we are talking about here is the work of self-cultivation. There's "heart-mind tending" to do. "Potency" here translates *de*. Having a heart-mind that is unswayed by circumstances is "the height of *de*". *De* is the existential realization of Dao. Dao is an attitude; *de* is having that attitude. Being "in the Dao" is *de*.

The goal and proof of this realization is to "rest content" in whatever transpires. However wonderful this might be, its most telling aspect is its everyday practicality. This is not about becoming a buddha. It is not about enlightenment, achieving immortality, or uniting with "the Great Dao". It's about enjoying one's life. The full realization of Dao, the *de* of Dao, is "resting content". Let's go out on a limb and call it: *happiness*.

What could be controversial about calling *de* happiness? Apart from its not promising some form of cosmic salvation or wowing spiritual charisma, it is often considered bad form to value happiness. What a mere *common* human aspiration! Mentioning it implies seeking it, and seeking it implies not having it, and it cannot be had by seeking—so abandon it. Just be an enlightened sage and have done with it. What does something so mundane as enjoying life have to do with supreme enlightenment, in any case?

And does not this passage itself tell us that resting content is not allowing "sadness and joy" to disturb our peace? Yes; happiness is not allowing happiness (or the need for or lack of happiness) to disturb our peace. What is missing in the critique above (besides a this-worldliness) is an appreciation of walking two roads at once. Paradox. Nothing in life is not paradoxical.

There is a hope that is a kind of non-hope, a hope that is an open-ended hopefulness that hopes for no *particular circumstance*. There is a sadness that is a kind of non-sadness, a sadness that does not overwhelm us; a sadness enjoyed as sadness. There is a happiness that requires no happiness; a happiness that equally embraces happiness and sadness. This is a happiness that depends on nothing— including happiness.

Resting content in every circumstance, including the circumstance of our emotional responses to them, is happiness. Since this is not in fact our natural inclination, all these circumstances (including the circumstance of our inability to do so) are an opportunity to "tend to our heart-mind". It's not about arriving, but about resting content in never arriving.

X

"Let yourself be carried along by things so that the mind wanders freely. Hand it all over to the unavoidable so as to nourish what is central within you. This is the most you can do." (4:16)

This morsel is found in "Confucius'" instructions to his disciple Yan regarding how to deal with a despotic ruler. Viewed from the side of volition, nearly everything this ruler has done was avoidable. However, this is no longer the case. It is done. It is now an unavoidable circumstance.

We have been considering the two greatest unavoidables we face, life and death. There are others—our inescapable existential dangle being chief among them. This is our inherent not-knowing while "needing" to know, our hunger for purpose where none can be found, and our desire for a continuity of identity where none can be seen to exist. Now we will consider those unavoidables that were previously avoidable but no longer are.

In many respects this species of the unavoidable offers an even more challenging opportunity for self-cultivation than does the former. Though we might rail against "heaven" for the necessary conditions of our existence, we could only do so as fully aware of the absurdity of the act. Our rebellion thus typically takes other, more subtle forms—principally religiously-minded forms that white-wash (purpose-wash) an otherwise uncompromising silence. What another mere mortal has brought about is likely to elicit an altogether different kind of response, however.

What someone does *to* me, directly or to others with whom I identify (hopefully everyone), or to the planet and its many life-forms with which I identify (hopefully)—this is likely to bring forth a whole different level of raw emotional responses. This is *personal*, damn it.

This is the everyday stuff of life. This is where the rubber meets the road. And this is where we find innumerable opportunities to imagine the peace of not taking offence at what is undeniably offensive.

XI

In a previous series I made reference to the proto-Daoist philosopher Song Xiang whom Zhuangzi lauds for his distinction between the inner and the outer, between how others behave toward us and how we behave toward ourselves. He is known for declaring that "to be insulted is not a disgrace". In other words, we need not be offended by offensive behavior directed our way. We need not be dependent on externals.

This behavior is something that has happened; it is now an unavoidable circumstance. However the various degrees of causation and culpability might be assigned, we are now in a position to "hand it all over to the unavoidable so as to nourish what is central within" us. We are in a position to take this unfortunate circumstance as an *opportunity* to do the work of self-cultivation.

This series arose from my recent ongoing experience with the IRS. I will spare you the details except to say that is manifests as a Kafkaesque tyranny oblivious to the rule of law. I get angry; and when I do, I try to say, "thanks for this opportunity." I try to do this with lots of things directed my way that I take to be harmful and unjust. I mention this, not to show myself as sagacious, but quite the opposite, as someone with lots of work to do.

Zhuangzi quotes Song Xiang as part of his argument for depending on nothing so as to wander free and easy through life. Nothing can harm you when you depend on nothing. We fear no loss when we have nothing to lose. These are hard sayings, and require a meditative investment to be appreciated. Appreciating them is getting the whole of Zhuangzi's vision. Might I suggest you try them, if only for the understanding? You need not fear the loss of your fears—they'll still be there when you get back.

The IRS would unjustly take a chunk of my retirement with the prospect of my eventually being penniless. So what? Apart from this all being a mere hypothetical circumstance (I find I worry a lot about what in fact never happens), nothing can harm me when everything is an opportunity for soaring.

Fortunately, walking two roads allows me to fight the bastards nonetheless.

XII

Zhuangzi uses Song Xiang's appeal for non-dependence on external circumstances as a hinge that turns to his suggested non-dependence on internal circumstances. Not only do the opinions and behaviors of others toward us not matter, but neither do our own self-opinions. Song's contrast is between a self-esteem that depends on what others think of us, and a self-esteem that is founded on our own self-assessment. Zhuangzi would have us abandon even that. No-self is having a self that requires no reifying projects at all; a self that does not need to be a self even as it enjoys being one. Consideration of what it means to fear the loss of nothing doesn't take long to arrive here: the loss of the fear of losing oneself. This, I believe, is Zhuangzi's no-self.

This is very much about self-image. How do I view myself? But viewing myself is not being myself; it is a mediating separation from myself; it is a relationship of dependence. No-self is unmediated self; spontaneous self; and that's a whole lot of self. It's free-self.

Whether we are proud of ourselves (I have a great ass; My team's number one; I'm really smart; I drive a Beemer; I'm a success; I'm a very spiritual person) or dis- ourselves, it amounts to the same thing—we have a dependent self, a self in need of props. And this, Zhuangzi suggests, is what chains us to fear and renders us incapable of happily and playfully skipping through life.

Yeah, well, that's all well and good, but it's not how we actually are. How we actually are is our present unavoidable circumstance whether we could theoretically be otherwise or not. But then this circumstance, like any other, is an opportunity to do a bit of self-cultivation. And this can be fun. It can occasion an enjoyable buzz. Transcendence feels good. And we can even transcend our inability to transcend—not eradicate it, but transcend it. Without pride and shame there would be nothing *to* transcend.

"Every enslavement is also an ennobling" (2:41).

XIII

I began this series by agreeing with Steve Coutinho (*An Introduction to Daoist Philosophies*) that the philosophically important word *ming* is better translated as "circumstance" than as "fate" or "destiny". This is because the latter two can easily be taken as connoting fatalism, determinism, or even purposiveness. Any of these would, for Zhuangzi, be saying far too much. For him, *ming* is simply the circumstances in which we find ourselves and with which we must interact whatever their source or "reason".

I have thus far been skirting the thorny issues of fatalism (the belief that what has happened *had* to happen) and determinism (the belief that we cannot change the course of events). Though the logical mind might want to insist that these come into play when Zhuangzi says "hand it all over to the unavoidable", I think otherwise. Ziporyn, in his defense of Guo Xiang's interpretation of Zhuangzi as not fatalistic, makes the point that a certain degree of self-contradiction is itself unavoidable. That's the way of it.

Here's the point: Total acceptance of what cannot be avoided (and I have stretched this to include absolutely *every* current circumstance however contingently determined) does not entail not trying to change their consequences.

We will most certainly die; we can, nonetheless, work toward longevity even as we appreciate that long life and short life are equally "good". ("No one lives longer than a dead child".) (The sages "delight in early death; they delight in old age; they delight in the beginning; they delight in the end".)

We can live carefree beneath the sword of tyranny (having nothing to lose), and still join the underground.

We can be free of self-condemnation, and still take responsibility for our actions when they negatively impact others.

We can realize how that all is ultimately well and perfect, and still work to make things better here "beneath Heaven", that is, in the human context.

CATCH THE FISH, FORGET THE TRAP
I - IV

I

There is an interesting dialogue in the first of the Inner Chapters of the *Zhuangzi* that I think can help us to get past literalism and closer to the actual spirit of what Zhuangzi has in mind. This applies not only to this passage, but also to much of his work as a whole.

Jian Wu, an apparent novice in things Daoist, relates the words of the madman Jieyu about a sage living on a holy mountain to the sage Lian Shu. Jian finds the words fantastic and ridiculous—unbelievable. Lian, however, chastises Jian for his spiritual blindness and goes on to further describe the amazing attributes of this sage.

For my part, I often refer to this account of an august sage as proof of the folly of taking Zhuangzi literally. Am I also spiritually blind? Perhaps. But maybe literalism is its own kind of blindness.

Here's part of that description: "There's a Spirit-Man living on distinct Mt. Guye with skin like ice and snow, gentle and yielding like a virgin girl. He does not eat the five grains but rather feeds on wind and dew. He rides upon the air and clouds, as if hitching his chariot to dragons, wandering beyond the four seas" (1:12).

I take the madman Jieyu as religiously credulous, Jian as too dense to see beyond the words, and Lian, as the voice of Zhuangzi, pushing the allegory still further. There are important things being said here, but they are not what is said. This is Zhuangzi having fun as a vehicle for sharing an experience that words really can't express.

II

The madman Jieyu apparently has no difficulty believing there is a sage who subsists on only wind and dew. Is this a problem? Zhuangzi doesn't suggest so; in fact his sage voice confirms this and more: "This man is harmed by no thing. A flood may reach the sky without drowning him; a drought may melt the stones and scorch the mountains without scalding him" (1:13).

But clearly this must be hyperbole. The alternative is to engage in religious credulity in the extreme. Instead, we can turn it all on its head and say that the sage starves for lack of anything to eat or drink but wind and dew, is drowned by flood, and is burnt up by drought— and yet it does not harm him. This points us to the very heart of Zhuangzi's vision, that we should so identify with the Great Happening—the "vastest arrangement"—that no happening can harm us. One with change, no change is unacceptable. This is "hiding the world in the world where nothing can be lost".

But again, is religious credulity a problem? It is only if we wish to realize Zhuangzi's vision. Rather than "handing it all over to the unavoidable", we would *depend upon* particular outcomes. We would believe in "benefit and harm"; our happiness and security would be conditional.

Ultimately, however, religious credulity is no problem at all. If we affirm and identify with the Totality, no expression is unacceptable. Religion is but another coping strategy, not ultimately different in kind than Zhuangzi's. It's really a question of which strategy we find most compatible with our experience.

III

When Zhuangzi uses the voice of a fictional sage to express his philosophy we are also invited to appreciate the fantastic character of what is said. Zhuangzi is a jokester and trickster. He wants us to "get it" without giving us something to get. If there were some propositional truth to believe in, we would be back "taking our minds as our teacher". "Just be empty, nothing more." Experiential Dao is described as "the Great Openness"; openness attaches to no one "truth" but wanders freely among them all. A great openness stretches the self out and beyond its self-contained self. Give it an imaginative try—it's easy enough.

Those familiar with Zen should have no problem appreciating this method. What is the Buddha? "A shit stick." "The courtyard tree." "Three pounds of flax." Woe to the disciple that thinks his mind can penetrate these impenetrable surds. There is an experience quite different than "understanding" on offer here.

The point of Zhuangzi's fantastic jokery is to align the method with the message. The method is the message. Having overturned the belief that dependence on the rationalizing mind can integrate us with the life experience, how could he then just dish out more of the same?

IV

The polar opposite of religious credulity is closed-minded disbelief. We can sympathize with Jian Wu's dismissal of the madman Jieyu's story of a sage who subsists on only wind and dew, but his scathing rebuke by the sage Lian Shu makes us think twice. "It is not only the physical body that can be blind and deaf; the faculty of understanding can also be so. If you were to then 'agree' with these words, you would be acting like a virgin girl who has just reached her time" (1:13).

"Agreeing" with this story would indeed be just religious credulity because Jian has no personal experience that could possibly justify him doing so. Belief in such sages—fully realized masters and the like—can become a surrogate for our own actual lives. "Spiritual" reality becomes something other than our own reality. Whatever path we might be on, the reality of it is our present experience, not some hypothetical ideal that is likely a chimera. This present experience is the truth of it. Authentic living is about right now, not tomorrow.

Jian is reminiscent of Huizi, Zhuangzi's Logician debating buddy. Huizi dismissed Zhuangzi's philosophy as "big and useless" because he couldn't think outside the box. There is an alternative beyond credulity and disbelief. There are imaginative exercises possible that neither believe nor disbelieve.

Huizi had a huge gourd which, when it proved too big for conventional uses as a water bottle or dipper, he smashed to bits. Why did he not use his imagination, asked Zhuangzi, and use it as a boat to wander on the rivers and lakes (a metaphor for spiritual freedom)?

Huizi had a vast stink tree from which nothing could be made, so he chopped it down. "Why not plant it in our homeland of not-even-anything, the vast wilds of open nowhere?" asked Zhuangzi. "Then you could loaf and wander there, doing lots of nothing there at its side, and take yourself a nap, far-flung and unfettered, there beneath it" (1:15)?

This is the "uselessness of the useless"; if only we can break out of the box of truth and untruth and see what possibilities lay beyond.

SCOTT P. BRADLEY

HUMAN NATURE
I – VII

I

In order to understand mountain gorillas we study their behavior. Through history, anthropology, and sociology we attempt to do the same with humans, but for obvious reasons fail to attain the same objectivity. Nor should we expect or aspire to do so; the complete objectification of anything is to close oneself off from the infinite mystery that everything is. Nevertheless, there is value in taking a sober look at things as they manifest.

The classical Chinese philosophers found it necessary to objectively consider the character of human nature because they were most concerned with societal change. How can we best collectively flourish given human nature? What is human nature? These inquiries arose in the Warring States period (475-221 BCE) when things weren't going so well. There was need for change, and the means to effect that change should be predicted on the essential character of humanity.

In this series I will be reflecting on the generalized responses of three philosophers (Mencius, Xunzi, and Zhuangzi) to this challenge. Mencius and Xunzi were Confucians and framed the question of human nature in moral terms. Are humans inherently good (harmonious with their collective flourishing) or evil (disharmonious)? They held to opposing views.

Zhuangzi did not think in terms of the moral character of humanity but rather thought that doing so was part of the problem. I will argue that his more "cosmic" perspective, his view from Dao, allowed him to approach the problem very much as we do when considering the behavior of mountain gorillas—phenomenologically.

Still, he was a human being and as such wished for the collective and individual flourishing of our species. He, too, was required to make assumptions about the ability of humanity to realize these ends, albeit in the light of a larger context which relativized the value of even that.

II

Mencius (c. 372-289 BCE), the first great interpreter of Confucius, had a relatively optimistic view of human nature. Yes, humanity has made a mess of things, but despite our inclinations toward disharmony, we remain good at the core. Humaneness—empathy and fellow-feeling—is naturally embedded in the human heart. Anyone seeing a child about to fall into a well, he argues, will immediately jump to prevent it from happening. Our spontaneous caring reveals our true nature.

Unfortunately, society has developed in such a way as to distance us from our inner humanity. We have learned to value individual wealth and fame above our communal flourishing. It's very much like a nearby mountain, he says. It was once covered with a beautiful forest, but over the years it has been so exploited by logging and goat herding that it is now a wasteland. Given time, the seeds of its goodness would sprout again and it would again flourish. Only, as soon as these sprouts arise, they are once again foraged by goats.

The answer to this disharmony is education as a form of moral cultivation. People can be taught to let their natural humanity predominate once again. I am not familiar enough with Mencius or Confucianism generally to say what formal structure this education was intended to take, but it seems enough to know what humanness is and to cultivate it in one's daily interactions with others.

This self-cultivation, because it looks within and attempts to reconnect with the inner self, lends itself to a form of mysticism. We experience ourselves through a release into ourselves beyond words.

It also follows that if human nature is good and what we want to express then Nature (Heaven, Everything) as a whole is also good. Reconnecting with our unmediated self-experience organically reconnects us with the Totality. It gives one a sense of joyous oneness. This is likely what Mencius experienced when he spoke of being overwhelmed by "flood-like *qi*" (vital energy).

We will continue this discussion of Mencius, especially as he might be compared to Zhuangzi, in the next post. In closing here, I would like to point out the simplicity of this model. Releasing into yourself you release into Everything. What could be more natural? What does one need to "know"?

III

Mencius, like Confucius, wanted to transform society and believed the best way to begin was through the education of individuals. The chief content of this teaching was how to live humanely, which is to say humanly. But this means that we can trust our humanity, our nature, to naturally harmonize with the world, ourselves, and others given the opportunity to do so. Human nature is essentially good. We must re-connect with our inner-most selves.

Given his unexplained reference to his experience of "flood-like *qi*", some have said that Mencius was more a mystic than Zhuangzi. By some definitions of mysticism, this may be true. We needn't, however, let such judgements obscure how they are very similar in their appreciation of the value of reconnecting with our precognitive selves. They differ in that, for Zhuangzi, this movement is not mediated by a belief in the "goodness" of human nature, but by its "isness". Nature, for Zhuangzi, does not make moral discriminations, a purely human activity. This does not mean that Mencius was mistaken or that the result of such a mystical reconnection with one's pre-cognitive self and through it with Nature itself does not lead to greater humaneness; it is simply that for Zhuangzi this outcome is incidental—a happy circumstance.

They may also differ in that Mencius may have thought of *qi* as a something. Typically, mysticism is defined as identification with something Other; and this would lend itself to thinking Mencius more a mystic than Zhuangzi whose mysticism turns on the emptiness of any concept of an Other. However, *qi* can also simply refer to Life and the life-experience, which is to say, an experienced mystery.

Zhuangzian mysticism does differ significantly from Mencius' (I believe) in that his rests entirely on an emptiness of content. To depend on nothing means to depend on no one interpretation of reality, and no morally-inspired program. Be like experienced Nature itself. Be yourself. Look into the night sky (like Camus' Stranger) and be like that. Vast and limitless. Morally indifferent. Now come back and live the particular, moral you.

IV

The Confucian Xunzi (Hsün Tzu, c. 310-c. 220 BCE) wrote of Zhuangzi that he knew a great deal about Heaven, but little about humanity; he was a "nook and cranny scholar", as the *Tianxia* chapter (33) of the *Zhuangzi* would have it. He, on the other hand, dismissed Heaven as irrelevant given our not knowing anything about it, and believed he understood humanity well enough to prescribe a cure for its ailments. What he did not understand of Zhuangzi, however, is that for him Heaven represents our omnipresent not-knowing which militates against all definitive prescriptions.

Xunzi took the opposite track of Mencius; he held that human nature tends toward disharmony and chaos. Though admitted as overly simplistic, these two are often juxtaposed as one declaring human nature good and the other as declaring it evil.

Philosophers enjoy Xunzi because he is among the first to actually attempt a systematic presentation of his philosophy. I like him for his clear antithesis to Daoist sensibilities and his wonderfully outrageous statements, one of which I paraphrase here: "Humans are by nature warped and must be straightened by use of straightening boards." Thank you, Xunzi!

Thus, whereas Mencius was able, in agreement with Daoist thinking, to advocate for a return to our most essential selves, Xunzi advocated for external restraints—laws, punishment and rewards, and totalitarian government (beneficent, of course!).

In terms of an assessment of the moral character of human nature, I lean more to the side of Xunzi. I'm rather pessimistic about the ability of humanity to behave "humanely" and intelligently. I offer history and our present circumstances as my only "proofs". (My belief in my own essential goodness I will keep to myself since it is likely shared by most others but nevertheless does not appear to radically affect the prevailing mayhem except perhaps as a limiting factor.) Unlike Xunzi, however, and thanks to Zhuangzi, this does not lead me to similar practical solutions.

Zhuangzi invites us to consider humanity as we would any other natural phenomenon. Is the Universe wonderful, or is it not? If chaos, impermanence, death and apparent meaninglessness are evil, then the Universe is evil and so is everything within it. If it is wonderful, then so also is all that happens within it. Such a happy saying. Such an impossibly hard saying. If we can break upon this moral stumbling-block, however, we can still return to our concern for our individual and collective flourishing without that requiring a mortifying fear of the "warped".

Affirming apparent reality requires a suspension of moral discrimination. Nature is not moral. This does not mean that we should not be moral, but only that our moral concerns can be understood in a wider context. To be released from the bondage of this addiction only means that we can now better enjoy and make better use of that to which we were previously addicted.

V

Zhuangzi's rebuttal to Xunzi's assertion that the former knew much about Heaven but little about humanity would likely be something like: Yea rather my brother, what I know from Heaven is that I do not know, and knowing that we do not know is the most important thing we can know about being human. (Some sticklers on the nature of Zhuangzi's skepticism would add that he does not know whether he knows or not.) This leads to an altogether different approach to the improvement of our admittedly dysfunctional individual and societal circumstances.

For Zhuangzi, as for most Chinese philosophers of his time, Heaven is essentially equivalent to Nature; it is not an active agent at work in the world, but simply represents the seemingly necessary larger context for apparent reality. Nature does not only refer to what "is", but to what lies behind its isness. The *Laozi*'s assertion that "Dao does nothing, yet nothing is left undone" puts this succinctly, albeit somewhat paradoxically.

In the previous post I declared that "Nature is not moral" and was subsequently asked if this was not itself a moral judgement. There is no lack of Daoist "authority" on this issue (*Laozi* 5: "Heaven and earth are not humane; they treat the things of the world as straw dogs. The sage is not humane; he treats the people as straw dogs."), but I do not wish to rely on authority. My reply was that the vulnerability of this statement resides more in the epistemological realm than the ethical. Declaring Nature to be *a*moral is quite different than declaring it to be moral or *im*moral. But still, how do I know this?

I do not. The best I can do is to say that it seems so. Nature does not appear to have any concern with moral issues and thus cannot be *taken* as lending any moral guidance to humanity. It is this last that was the real issue for Zhuangzi—our moral judgements, whatever their value to humanity, do not objectively derive from Heaven and thus no appeal can be made to Divine authority or to any fixed and sure standard. Our moral judgements are species, culturally, and individually relative. (So let's loosen up on things upon which we do not have universal agreement.) This is important to Zhuangzi primarily in that it can help release us into non-dependence and free and carefree wandering. The world could go to hell in a handbasket, and the sage along with it, but still her joy would not be diminished even as she works to avoid such an end.

In the end, declaring Heaven to be moral or immoral would be "adding to the process of life" and fleeing "the illumination of the obvious". Understanding Heaven to be amoral is equivalent to admitting that one does not know anything beyond the seemingly obvious, which is a purely practical kind of knowledge.

VI

Before giving a brief summary in the post to follow of what I believe Zhuangzi's position on the character of human nature is, it might be helpful to suggest what it is not, whatever its character. "Human nature" does not mean "innate nature" (*hsing/xing*), a term that is not found in the Inner Chapters of the *Zhuangzi* or the *Laozi*, and only appears in the 3rd Century BCE. The difference is that the former speaks phenomenologically—it is descriptive of the human expression—the latter is essentialist—it reifies the human self-experience, makes it a something, and gives us something to believe in.

Does this matter practically? Perhaps not; but since I personally understand Zhuangzi's entire vision to pivot on radical non-dependence on any fixed reality or idea, this belief, should it become the object of self-cultivation—an attempt to discover or realize one's "true nature"—then it can only serve to hinder his appeal to complete openness (=emptiness). Human nature is how we behave, not what we essentially "are".

VII

Zhuangzi was in no way a systematic philosopher. "Vague! Ambiguous!" (33; p 124) He did not definitively weigh in on any cosmological or ethical issues. This was by design, and leaves his readers to come to their own conclusions. Thus, "The guidelines within them [his writings] are undepletable, giving forth new meanings without shedding the old ones".

We cannot therefore make definitive statements regarding his position vis-à-vis the character of human nature. We can only deduce a position after considering his larger concerns and advocacy. But even here we must remember that he wished to go beyond the need for any such declarations. We want it to all fit together and make good sense. We want a system, and he suggests we free ourselves from this need. We want a moral system, and he tells us that this stands in the way of our being truly moral. A prescriptive morality is an oppressive morality. And counter-productive. Witness the desire of the religious to impose their values on others despite the harmlessness of the behaviors in question.

On my reading, Zhuangzi suggests we reconnect with our most immediate and unmediated self-experience. Life does not ask Why? It simply lives. So, live. Life is its own enjoyment. So, enjoy. On this basis we can assume that Zhuangzi believes that human nature is "good" in a non-ethical sense. Whether we do "good" or "evil" is of only secondary importance. We do best when we trust Nature as it arises. Questions regarding the ethical belong to an altogether different sphere (road). As some Zennist has said, concern for morality simply evinces a continued bondage to morality.

But we want to know that this all leads to moral behavior. Like a scratched record, we inevitably fall back into the same groove. So here's the song in my groove: Zhuangzi suggests we become sages— is a sage an immoral person? Perhaps Zhuangzi's Daoism should come with a warning: Performed by a sage—do not try this at home. In other words, don't put the cart before the horse. Let your amorality arise from your growth in non-dependent sagacity. My guess is that that will make you very moral in the eyes of the world.

HAVING A GOOD LAUGH
I – IV

I

Though laughter might seem a rather superficial human activity, both psychology and (some) philosophies make much of it. The types of humor that give rise to laughter are many and we needn't consider them all here, except by way of a fundamental contrast. Sardonic, sarcastic and other species of humor that deprecate others or oneself are not germane to the topic here.

Since our point of departure is the philosophy of Zhuangzi, it is his humor that inspires this treatment. Zhuangzi does not tell explicit jokes, and yet the entirety of his writing can be taken as just that—a kind of joke. This is not incidental, but intentional and integral to his message.

After sharing the fantastic story of an incredibly vast fish that transforms into a huge bird that ascends to forty thousand feet in order to fly to some distant Oblivion, he tells us that it can be found in a certain book that Ziporyn translates as "*The Equalizing Jokebook*". (1:3) He tells us in a note (3) that it could also be "*The Equalizing Harmony*". I prefer the former; but in either case it is probably itself a joke in that he likely made the name up. The fictional and fantastic is proved by referencing an authoritative source which is itself fictional. What are we to believe?

I take the entirety of the Inner Chapters as just that, an Equalizing Jokebook; and he may very well have wished us to make that connection.

So, what's the joke? The joke is that something we might have taken very seriously is conveyed so unseriously that we are led to question whether it was ever all that serious after all. It all seems so tongue-in-cheek. Rather than coming away with definitive answers, we are cast into further doubt.

Still, there seems to be something serious being said here. But it is something that can best be seen only if we look peripherally—very much like objects in the dark are better seen when not looked at directly. The use of humor is thus a kind of "indirect method"—an indefinite, but suggestive pointing. It is a kind of "wordless instruction".

II

Zhuangzi's humor is basically ironic. Ironic humor typically turns on the incongruity of a statement with perceived "facts". It states the opposite of what we likely believe to be the case so as to make us actively reconsider and (probably) recommit to that belief, though now some ambiguity has entered the equation. We are required to engage in a process. This is often good for a chuckle.

Irony can take different forms.

On a sweltering day I can say, It's hot. Or I can ask, Is it hot enough for you? This latter requires you to think about it and come to your own conclusion that yes, it's hot as hell. When Zhuangzi poses the possibility of depending on nothing we are similarly required to engage in an imaginative exercise.

A classic example of an ironic situation is seen when an Athenian general consults the Oracle on the eve of battle, and asks about the outcome. "There will be a great victory," is the reply. He thus confidently engages in battle only to discover that that victory belongs to the opposing general. He failed of a sense of irony—the ability to see the ambiguity inherent in all things and to avoid literalism.

Then there is the case of Socrates who was told that the Oracle had declared him the wisest man in the world. Since he knew he knew so little, he made it his mission to prove the Oracle wrong by questioning those who "knew" what he did not. The mission itself was ironic, of course, since he knew that not-knowing was the source of his wisdom. But his ironic questioning served to awaken others to their own not-knowing and to perhaps become a bit wiser thereby.

Zhuangzi brazenly declares the fantastic, the obviously fictional, and historical truth bent to his purposes to make us consider and engage with possibilities that lie beyond what can be said.

III

As already suggested, an ironic statement requires thoughtful engagement in order to be understood. Yet, when understood, there is no sure form that that understanding will take. It is a subjective truth.

This, of course, is an example of *wu-wei*, non-being the change. It is pedagogical midwifery. The midwife does her part to be sure, but the real work is done by she who delivers, and that which she delivers is uniquely her own.

This reflects the Daoist position on the exercise of power generally. The ruler rules in such a way that when there are positive outcomes the people declare, "We did it ourselves." (*Laozi* 17) She yins. Yet most rulers and teachers want to be in full control so as to be sure of the results and to be able to take credit for them. They yang.

Taken ironically, the Inner Chapters do not guarantee a single interpretation. "The guidelines within them are undepletable, giving forth new meanings without shedding the old ones. Vague! Ambiguous! We have not got to the end of them yet." (33; p 124)

The real parting of ways when interpreting Zhuangzi is found here. Are we to take it all literally, or do we understand it as only a vague pointing? Is it yang, or is it yin? Does it tell us the truth of things, or does it help us to find our own truth?

The ability to rest in this ambiguity and its consequently diverse "truths" is in itself part of the purpose of this Zhuangzian joke. It is Dao as the confluence of all daos and the ability to "go by the presence of the present 'this'." (2:16)

"For him [the sage], each thing is just so, each thing is right, and so he enfolds them all within himself by affirming the rightness of each." (2:41)

IV

Tiny birds laugh derisively at the flight of the mighty Peng. Their laughter evinces their egoic closed-mindedness. Their narrow experience is the measure of all things. Song Xing laughs at those who, like the birds, commit to their petty accomplishments as sufficient to make them "someone". He is "better" than they. (1:7)

The sage laughs joyously in the freedom of play. Her laughter is celebratory. She "takes part everywhere as the springtime of each being". (5:16) Her laughter is an affirming appreciation of every expression.

A Zennist who has just experienced satori declares: All that's left is to have a good laugh. How so? Previously, all was so serious; there was a self to be saved. Now, all is well and is seen to have always been so.

But why laugh? Laughter turns on incongruity; all these messes, this Great Mess, are recontextualized in an experience of unconditional Wellness. This laughter evinces transcendence.

But transcendence is not negation. The messes remain. Indeed, without them there would be no transcendence, nor occasion for laughter.

We have before us a picture of a bloodied child, irredeemably traumatized by war. Shall we laugh? Can we laugh still? We cannot laugh at this, but we still laugh, do we not? Or do we descend into an abyss of anguished despair? What is it then that allows us to live on—to laugh with our own children, to enjoy the bitter-sweet of life?

Some may be scandalized by a declaration of universal Wellness—but they live it just the same. Life itself is hopefulness and trust. Hope dawns eternal because life itself is irredeemably celebratory.

IDOLATRY
I – IV

I

"What is an idol? Any god *who is mine but not yours*, any god concerned with me but not with you, *is an idol*." –Rabbi Abraham Heschel, "RELIGION AND RACE" (14 January, 1963)

Concern about idolatry may seem tangential to a study of Zhuangzi's Daoism, but when we understand it as any act that establishes a circumscribed coherence that must necessarily exclude other coherences, it speaks directly to the overall vision of Zhuangzi. Everything said leaves out something else—and that absence becomes the most important thing of all. We cannot say or understand without it being a prelude to idolatry.

Why is the left out the most important thing of all? In a world of ceaseless Yang-ing, it is only Yin that can frame the whole. But Yin is Mystery—the unframeable.

The Daoist appeal for the inclusion of Yin/Dao is a call to openness. It is an appeal to let everything "bask in the broad daylight of Heaven". Openness is a synonym for emptiness. It is not a void, but a voiding. It has its point of departure, its yang, and it does not eradicate itself. The inclusion of Yin is not the exclusion of Yang.

Taking Dao for Something is idolatry. It is circumscribing (drawing a circle around) Openness. It is simply more Yang-ing. True Openness is an experience, not an idolatrous idea.

II

If there is a problem with idolatry from the point of view of Zhuangzian Daoism it is primarily in that it robs us of the opportunity to experience a sense of openness and limitlessness. These correspond to emptiness in that they are not in any sense definitively specifiable events—there is no "thing" called limitlessness. These terms must self-efface to retain their meaning.

Again, Zhuangzi believes that such an experience makes for a happier life. That's the whole of it.

Openness, to my thinking, can be taken as the whole of Zhuangzi's vision—just as it can be understood as synonymous with the goals of other similar approaches. I will attempt a quote from possibly the earliest Daoist/Zen treatise, *Xin-Xin Ming*, from a faulty memory: "Openness is easy; just hold no opinions about anything." Here also is one from a more secular source: "Nothing is more conducive to peace of mind than not having any opinion at all." (Georg Carl Lichtenberg).

Easy? I think not. Possible? Who knows? But certainly well worth the effort to explore its psychological and practical implications. Like so many characterizations of the psychology of sagacity, the first-order value of this one resides in its direct challenge to our typical inclinations. It rubs us the wrong way in a variety of ways, and that is our opportunity to explore the why of it. We needn't even have to agree with it to get an inkling of openness in considering it.

The introductory quote (I) inspired this series and it speaks to the practical and social consequences of openness that I will consider anon.

III

"What is an idol? Any god *who is mine but not yours*, any god concerned with me but not with you, *is an idol*." –Rabbi Abraham Heschel, "RELIGION AND RACE" (14 January, 1963)

This quote tells us that what excludes is idolatrous. Any conception of God that excludes is idolatrous. But this also implies that any conception of God at all is essentially idolatrous. To say, "This is God; these are His (!) attributes," is an act of identifying God within limits that exclude. This need not lead us to a definitive conclusion that there is no God; atheism is as idolatrous and exclusionary as any other absolutist belief.

What we are left with is utter not-knowing. All is Mystery and therefore every "thing" is existentially adangle and itself mystery.

The rational mind nevertheless works by virtue of its ability to include and exclude. We know what something is by knowing what it is not. Is this a sheep or a goat? It's a goat, because sheep have this attribute, while goats do not. The mind is dualistic by its nature.

Recognizing the essential Mystery that is our life-in-a-world enables us to open up into the totality of our experience without excluding anything. This experiential opening up is, to my thinking, what Zhuangzi is about when he speaks of Oneness. He treads very carefully here, however. Saying all is One is just another absolutist, and therefore exclusionary, statement. Oneness is an experience, not an explicit fact. Thus, he also says, "Not-One is also One".

Once again we find ourselves on two roads at once. By virtue of our experience as self-aware, rational beings we participate in a required dualism. Yet we also have the possibility of a non-dual experience that informs our dualism. We are by nature exclusionary, especially as evinced in our addiction to good and bad, but we can inform this with a broader experience that, though it does not negate our not-oneness, can render it non-absolutist. We can open up to our unopeness and realize some openness in that.

IV

"What is an idol? Any god *who is mine but not yours*, any god concerned with me but not with you, *is an idol*." –Rabbi Abraham Heschel, "RELIGION AND RACE" (14 January, 1963)

Hate is possible for the same reason that love is possible. Both require two. But this is not hard to find since twoness describes our most fundamental experience as self-aware beings. Self is "I" aware of itself as an "other", its "me".

Self-hatred may be the most common form of hatred, but finding itself too hard to bear, it projects itself onto more distant "others". The racism implied in the quote above likely has its beginnings here. Hate is exclusionary.

Love is inclusionary. It spans the gulf of twoness in the formation of a oneness. But this requires a twoness that is also a oneness, or a oneness that is also a twoness. How is it that everything always seems to speak of walking two roads at once?

Self-love must also be a formation of a oneness. Perhaps this can tell us something of what Ziqi meant when he said he'd lost his "me". He experienced himself as a twoness that was also a oneness. And this led him to a vision of the oneness of the forest by virtue of the self-so uniqueness of its trees. A Oneness that was also a not-Oneness.

Some degree of self-love must be a prerequisite to other-love. The more self-oneness, the more self-other-oneness. Fortunately, imperfection and approximation, which is to say the essential messiness of existence, manages to flourish despite the same.

This trajectory into inclusionary openness, oneness, is a central part of Zhuangzi's vision. I guess we could call it love, though he does not call it such. In any case, like love, it feels good. Perhaps this is something of what Buddhism is about when it speaks of all-inclusive compassion, though I've never quite got this supreme valuation of compassion. "Heaven is not humane." That's more my cup of tea.

Their real point of divergence, it seems to me, is that Buddhism seems to think this apparent reality needs saving by way of compassion, while Zhuangzian Daoism recognizes no such need. All is well in the Great Mess. Improving the experience is elective and can thus be accomplished playfully and without its being yet another burden.

YIN/YANG
I – VI

I

It took me a long time to warm up to yin and yang. The stench of religious belief and metaphysical hocus-pocus was just too strong. But I have clearly had a change of heart; though I have only really just taken them for my own purposes. And still I have not studied their uses in Chinese philosophy in any significant depth. I cannot, therefore, pretend to represent them in their traditional meanings or contexts. But that, of course, has never hindered my blabbering in other instances.

It might be good to begin by saying that there are no doubt lots of very helpful and insightful aspects to yin/yang philosophy even when embedded in the stinkiest of beliefs. And I have obviously profited from them.

Zhuangzi only explicitly speaks of yin and yang three times, and each time through the mouth of another and only in a reference to "internal yin and yang", a principle in Chinese medical theory.

Some commentators have suggested that they are together one of the "six atmospheric breaths" (*qi*) upon which the sage chariots in her wandering. (1:8) For the purpose of establishing my point of departure, let's assume that they are.

The sage wanders in non-dependence, and this renders all things and circumstances equal and interchangeable. If there were things or cosmic principles called yin and yang, the sage would have no need of them except as something upon which to "ride atop". But she can do that with any- and everything. They are interchangeable. This is her freedom.

211

The existence or non-existence of a metaphysical yin and yang is therefore absolutely moot. Just as the existence of metaphysical Dao or *qi* (*ch'i*) is moot.

In my usage, therefore, yin and yang are terms descriptive of psychological orientations. They are no more "real" than any other dialectic—they "exist" only as descriptive of a relationship between things.

There is value, however, in making reference to a hypothetical yin and yang as cosmic principles, just as there is in referencing metaphysical Dao. Dao is the big Question Mark—not the big Answer. This is its value. So too with yin and yang—they are useful concepts by which to interpret the world, but only as long as we do not render them substantively "real".

Now, after all this yanging I'm ready for some yinning.

II

At the heart of the Daoist revolution is the embrace of yin. Yin is what lies beyond the ever-receding horizon of our understanding, our yanging. It is that which unavoidably contextualizes all we think and experience in Mystery. It is that which is always left out, no matter how grand our pronouncements about Reality. It is the not-God beyond God.

What is left out, Zhuangzi tells us, is the most important thing of all. This is the discovery of Daoism. It is only the most important thing because it is left out. It has no other value. Were it to have some other value, it would be yang. It is not something yet to be discovered—Dao, God, I AM, Brahman, true self, true purpose—but the emptiness of Mystery.

Yin *is* Mystery. And Mystery has no content.

The *Laozi* is often represented as the first extant locus of this radical philosophical pivot toward yin. This may or may not be the case, but Zhuangzi's understanding may have been more radical still. This is a matter of interpretation; but the glorious first chapter of the *Laozi* seems to invite taking Non-Being as ultimate Yin in contrast to the Yang of Being. If this is the case, then this yin has been properly yanged. Yin (at this level) is the opposite of nothing—not even yang.

The embrace and prioritization of yin is not motivated by a belief that it is "higher", "better", or "more real". It is because we are by nature all about yang. We tend to forget our embedding in yin. And this makes for psychological dissonance. And this diminishes our enjoyment of life.

And that, to my thinking, is Zhuangzian Daoism's highest value, however parochial and prosaic that may seem.

III

Dao is ultimate Yin. Everything else both yins and yangs. Dao does nothing—it is Emptiness. We can say nothing more about "it". It has no content. It is, as I have said, the big Question Mark, not the big Answer.

In Daoism water is symbolic of yin. It follows the path of least resistance. It yields. Yet in the process it wears down the hardest rock. It occupies the lowest places. But then in wearing and occupying it also yangs. Everything both yins and yangs.

This is of utmost importance in the context of Daoism's psychological prioritization of yin. The goal is a realization of balance, not the eradication of yang. The implication is that typically we are *not* in balance. We have become excessive yangers.

The root cause of this is that we have taken our selves as "full and real". We wish to be ultimate Yang. Immortal. The alternative renders us a passing phenomenon. The core Zhuangzian experience of realizing that we "have not-yet-begun-to-exist", of "just being empty", is thus the yinning of our yang. We are exhorted to identify with Transformation instead of a concrete, static self.

But then no-self is not no self; that would be the eradication of yang. No-self is the self free from belief in a reified self. It is yang recontextualized in yin. It is the realization of balance.

The ultimate value here is simply to enjoy being the self that we are—to get the most out of the fleeting experience of our "temporary lodging".

IV

I often represent yin and yang as verbs. In their practical expressions this is what they are—activities. (It's also fun to create a bunch of neologisms, especially when they require the mind to think in new ways.)

Yin is an activity? Yang is doing, being, self-asserting—it is the essence of activity. How then can yin, its opposite, also be an activity? It is something we choose to do. We are what we do—we are a doing. We are unavoidably doers in every instance. If I decide to do nothing, then that it what I do. Though the goal of spontaneity is unmediated doing, it is doing nonetheless.

This is *wuwei*—not-doing. *Wuwei* is an activity informed of yin. *Wuwei* is a healthy balance of yin and yang.

In pedagogical midwifery, teaching has a goal and is an activity. It yangs. But it also yins. It is the yin of the method that makes it an expression of *wuwei*. Yin is the vacuous space that calls forth the yang.

This parallels Zhuangzi's unique take on *qi* (*ch'i*). You want to accumulate more *qi*? "Just be empty, nothing more." "*Qi* is an emptiness, a waiting for the presence of beings." (4:9) This *qi* is yin. Like water, its power resides in its yielding.

Yet *qi* is often represented as yang—an accumulation of a *something*, with a subsequent endowment of power. It may be (if it exists at all). But like the yanging of water, this happens only incidental to its yinning.

As inveterate yangers, we turn every call to yin into still more yanging. Even Dao becomes ultimate Yang.

V

Yang is light. Yin is darkness. Yang is knowing. Yin is not-knowing. Yang is positive. Yin is negative. Yang is life. Yin is death.

All these are reversible, of course. "Reversal is the movement of the Dao." (*Laozi* 40) This means that they can all be equalized and "united to form a oneness." Psychological Dao is realizing this oneness. Yet not-oneness remains. "Realizing" is by nature dualistic. As the convergence of all daos, Dao is both oneness and not-oneness.

Life and death taken as a single thread is the realization of this oneness. They are equalized. The sage is thankful for both. She welcomes life's coming and its going. This is the uniting of yin and yang to form a oneness. She therefore is able to make the best use of each in their not-oneness. The use of life is living and the enjoyment of life. The use of death is ... .

What is the use of death? Death is the looming of Yin. It is the contextualization of our yang in yin. Yin, darkness, sheds light on our yang.

We are caught in this vise, this existential dangle. All of Zhuangzi's philosophy can be seen as a response to death, an embrace of this yin. There is no escape; there are only coping mechanisms. From the human perspective, this is at the heart of messiness. It probably didn't have to be; the universe could have remained self-consciousness free. But it happened. Accidentally—for all practical purposes. Now we are left to live with it.

Thus, yin and yang can themselves be united to form a oneness. But in our not-oneness they are very useful dualistic concepts by which to orient ourselves in the world.

VI

These posts are obviously a lot of yanging. They make positive declarations about the nature of things.

I do sometimes try to put an empty edge on things—usually in the form of a question—something that will invite the reader to think outside their box and mine—but in the end, it's admittedly an excessive lot of yanging. Perhaps this is unavoidable. Words are a yanging.

It must be the reader, therefore, who supplies a balancing lump of yin. Doubt, if it furthers the process, is some of that yin. Certainly belief, taking things as unambiguously the case, only leads to being thoroughly yanged.

The Inner Chapters are also unavoidably a yanging. But, as I frequently note (in agreement with their own testimony and that of their later interpreters), they are presented in such a way as to also be a yinning. If "the radiance of drift and doubt is the sage's only map" (2:29), then it is understandable that the medium by which sagacity is presented also be ambiguous.

I have often spoken to this, and a series on Words will speak to it still further.

ON BEING SELF-SO (*ZIRAN*)
I – VIII

I

I begin this series with some trepidation. Though most all I write here goes beyond my actual scholarly knowledge (not to mention experience), this that follows can only be more so. The concept of *ziran*, typically translated "spontaneity", but more literally as "self-so", is too complex for me to imagine that I can do it justice. For this reason I will, in this case especially, fall back on the comforting fuzziness of calling these *reflections*.

I have been accused (by an off-blog commenter) of being overly influenced by the philosophy of Guo Xiang (252-312) (who made much of self-so) in my interpretation of Zhuangzi. This may be true. But let us assume that our every take-away from Zhuangzi is necessarily interpretive and that, therefore, there is no *definitive* Zhuangzi for us to discover. In that case, the "overly" in "overly influenced" loses much of its power to censure.

The ambiguity of Zhuangzi is intentional. Why? Think about it. If it were otherwise, he would have betrayed his own philosophy. We are required to engage with him as he would have us engage with life—in the context of an unavoidable adriftedness. We will nowhere discover a safe and sure "holding ground" wherein to plant our existential anchor. Better (happier) to enjoy the drift.

Let go the mooring;
Loose the lines.
The great void awaits—
A vast and empty sea.
—Chen Jen

II

Self-so means that everything spontaneously self-arises. This is equivalent to saying that everything has one foot in existence and the other in nothingness. Together, they represent the experience of emptiness, the experience of being a something that is also a nothing.

"Self-arising" means that nothing *causes* anything to happen—nothing is *caused*—things simply happen of themselves. This seems so counter-intuitive that we might be inclined to dismiss it out-of-hand. Perhaps the best way to consider such a possibility, therefore, is to simply take it as a thought experiment—an imaginative journey into the world of unlogic. But, be careful, you might just get dizzy and take an existential tumble.

It is common to think of metaphysical Dao as "the Source"—the First Cause, the Unmoved Mover. It's all a great Mystery, but it's *There*; the Mystery is Something. Not so, says Guo Xiang. Dao is quite literally *nothing*. (I would suggest that rather than such an absolutist statement we might instead say, Dao is *for all practical purposes* nothing.) Part of his argument for this position, as inspired by his reading of Zhuangzi, is that, if we follow the *idea* of causation back through time, we end up in an infinite regress. It's turtles all the way down. Unless, of course, we decide to stop at an Uncaused Cause, the Source, God... But what is this, he asks, if not Self-so and Self-arising? Why not rather accept that all things are themselves self-so and self-arising? All happenings are not simply consequential *parts* of the Great Happening—they *are* the Great Happening. There is no space here for causation.

So what? If this has no practical impact for our being-in-the-world, it's not worth the blabber. But it does make a difference, and I shall attempt to demonstrate how in the course of this series.

Guo Xiang was part of a movement known as *xuanxue* ("abstruse learning"), or as it has come to be known, "Neo-Daoism". The other famous exponent of this renewed interest in Daoism as philosophy was Wang Bi (226-249) whose commentary on the *Laozi* made much of the distinction between Being and Non-Being. Oh boy! Metaphysics! This very much appeals to reasoning mind, and thus to philosophy, because, for all its non-being-ness, Non-Being is still *something*. Dao is Non-Being and we can rest assured that there is something there for us to think about and cling to. Guo Xiang saw through this sleight-of-mind.

I mention this difference to illustrate how our "natural human inclination" is to posit the "reasonable" so as to make the world make "sense". Breaking these fetters was very much a part of Zhuangzi's vision of realizing freedom to wander. "Just release the mind to play..."

III

Guo makes several arguments for all things being self-so, uncaused and self-arising. We have already looked at the problem of infinite regress created by the idea of causation, and its only solution being a beginning that is uncaused, which is to say the *self-so*-ness we were trying to avoid in the first place. Thus, "Heaven" is not a causative something other than all things, but precisely all things. There are not-two (heaven and earth); and where there is not-two, there is no causation.

Another of his arguments is that nothing cannot cause something. He takes Non-Being as meaning what it actually implies—nothing. How can nothing cause something?

Arguments have their uses, but we must be wary of *depending* on them. Anything *proven* true is existentially *un*true. Zhuangzi makes similar arguments that inspired Guo's, but his differ fundamentally in intent. All he wanted to prove is that we can prove nothing. (Gotcha! This is self-contradictory! Exactly!) We are existentially a-dangle. This leads us to the examination of our actual experience so that we might harmonize our living with life, which, quite frankly, makes no sense. Get over it. That's Zhuangzi's vision in a nutshell—getting over it—getting so far over it that life becomes a playful romp.

I promised that I would show how this is something practically helpful, something more than just speculative blabber. I cannot—showing it would just amount to more blabber. I can, however, recommend an imaginative excursion into the possibility of your being the Great Happening. Not part of an endless line of caused events whose sum is the Great Happening, but the Great Happening as not-two. This is "hiding the world in the world"—not a Truth, but an activity. Not knowing, but living.

IV

There are two principal ways in which Zhuangzi suggests that reality presents as self-so (spontaneously arising)—cosmologically and existentially. Dao and self are both noticeable for their absence. They are present only through their absence. All we can say of the cosmos and ourselves is that they appear to happen. We can discover no cause, nor any rhyme or reason for their happening. Stuff just happens. Existence seems to have spontaneously arisen without any substantive Ground of Being anchoring it to Meaning.

Ziqi explains the loss of his "me" through the analogy of the "piping of Heaven": "It gusts through all the ten thousand differences, allowing each to go its own way. But since each one selects out its own [way], what identity can there be for their rouser?" (2:5) "Dao does nothing, yet nothing is left undone".

The absence of an identifiable cause for things to have arisen is echoed in our inability to discover a substantive self in ourselves. There's no one home. True self is no-self, which is to say, it is the realization by one's self that it has no reified "soul". It "is" only as an "is not". It is a something that is also a nothing. Losing one's "me" is this realization. The loss of one's "me" as that which makes us "other" to ourselves and to all "other selves" is, ironically, precisely what allows us a sense of oneness with all things. We're all in this together—one big Happening.

Our most immediate experience of being self-so is this experience of being ungrounded. Rather than asking why we are here, a reason the "understanding consciousness" requires to its own disquiet, realizing ourselves as self-so, as spontaneously arising, sets the stage for living as such—spontaneously.

V

Ziporyn entitled his book on Guo Xiang's philosophy "The Penumbra Unbound", an allusion to a story in Chapter 2 of the *Zhuangzi* and repeated in 27 with some interpretative emending. It is in his commentating here that Guo makes his strongest argument for all things being self-so, uncaused and self-arising. This is the story of a shadow's conversation with its own shadow. The topic is why Shadow does what it does. Penumbra (the shadow of Shadow) wants to know. A third party, the ostensible concrete *cause* of Shadow, is only vaguely implied, seemingly irrelevant. Penumbra seems to assume its own non-dependence on Shadow; it only questions the reasons for Shadow's behavior but not its own, just as we typically assume our own volitional independence. Everything has a sense of its own non-dependence.

This story is about the possibility of a *psychological* release from the bonds of dependence as represented in the concept of causation. Utter psychological non-dependence, in my view, is the primary experiential expression of Zhuangzi's vision for free and carefree wandering. Causation is but another word for dependence. Thus, just as we can realize non-dependence *despite* our being utterly *dependent* in every way, so too can we realize ourselves as non-caused (self-so) despite our being in every way caused. I hope that the word "transcendence" can help to make sense of this apparent nonsense.

The story preceding this one has a character allude to Ziqi's analogy of the response to the wind by the trees: "Even though the transforming voices may depend on one another, this is tantamount to not depending on anything at all" (2:45). They are all one in their transforming, identified with Transformation. Non-dependence is not *in*dependence, but a psychological transcendence of all dependence facilitated by our trustful release into the whatever-may-happen of Mystery.

Similarly, realizing oneself as self-so, spontaneously arising, is not a denial of causation, but its transcending.

Our scientific-mindedness stumbles at this transcendence of causation, but it is curious that if we were discussing free-will—the ability to make choices that are not absolutely *determined*—we would not be quite so reticent. Even Zhuangzi and Guo could be seen as ultimately asserting determinism—we do what we are, we perfectly accomplish what we are. Yet, even in this, is a vast freedom—the freedom to be what we cannot help but be:

"[E]very being without exception is released into the range of its own spontaneous attainments, so that each being relies on its own innate character, each deed exactly matching its own capabilities. Since each fits perfectly into precisely the position it occupies, all are equally far-reaching and unfettered" (Guo Xiang; p 129).

VI

Lift your hand and you'll likely see its shadow. Imagine it as just as "real", substantial and free as your hand. Stand in the sunlight and consider that sense in which your shadow is as real and free as you are. ("Seen from the point of view of their sameness, all things are one.") Our reluctance to do so is precisely what's happening in the story of Penumbra questioning the shadow of which it is the shadow, only in the reverse.

We think of our shadow as utterly dependent upon our own existence and activities. It disappears the moment we step into the shade. It sits when we sit and stands when we stand. Nothing could be more obviously the case. But our shadow might laugh and ask of us how we are any different. How are we any less dependent? Do we not also depend upon an infinite number of conditions in order to exist? Do we know why we do what we do—truly? How are we any less ephemeral? Does duration make a difference? Is the tree Mingling that lives for thousands of years less ephemeral than the morning mushroom that knows nothing of noon? ("No one lives longer than a dead child".) From the point of view of our shadow, we are essentially the same.

Only in Zhuangzi's story, Penumbra, like ourselves, assumes its own independence while questioning that of Shadow of which it is the shadow. Where things are united to form a oneness (the imaginative exercise of dao-izing the world), all opposites become reversible. ("Not-One is also One".) Penumbra is fully aware of its own transcendent self-arising—sits when it wants to sit, stands when it wants to stand—but wonders about that of Shadow. The standing and sitting human being, who casts the Shadow of which Penumbra is the shadow, does not even merit a mention despite our thinking it the prime mover. He must be utterly determined, dependent and inconsequential. Yet, "Reversal is the movement of the Dao"—dao-ing is the ability to reverse and to thereby "unite to form a oneness". *Even* the human being is as self-so as the shadow of its shadow.

Ziporyn has suggested that Zhuangzi sees all things as having a point of view. If we insist that this requires self-awareness, then this makes no sense at all. But if we grant things their own self-so emergence, then we are obliged to grant them that which we assign to ourselves. Having self-arisen, all things that "are" "seek" to continue to "be". "Each selects out its own [way]."

So what? We explore this in the next post.

VII

Zhuangzi thinks it is important to squarely face our experience of the absence of any knowable First Cause, Dao, or Source. Positing a Something that makes sense of life is giving the mind priority over our existential experience. And this is an act of "bad-faith", a flight from our own humanity. It sets us on a path of inauthentic living. Where life as it has evolved in us seems to require mechanisms for coping, however, even this inauthenticity has its advantages. Belief is a powerful opiate, and we are in no position to deny people what they have chosen for the alleviation of their pain. Zhuangzi's vision is simply for an alternative response to the life-experience, one that he believes leads to a greater enjoyment of life.

Zhuangzi is far from being an atheist. How could he possibly take such an absolutist position? We might call him an agnostic, but this still suggests an abiding in the realm of *gnosis*, knowing. His not-knowing is not about epistemology, but serves as a point of departure into a more immediate and primal experience of life. His agnosticism has wings. His flight is into Openness. And Openness allows life to freely flow in us as the whatever-it-is.

Such an experience is what he calls the Numinous Reservoir, the inexplicable experience of the self-arising of life within us. "That is what allows the joy of its harmony to open into all things without thereby losing its fullness, what keeps it flowing on day and night without cease, taking part everywhere as the springtime of each being. Connecting up with This, your mind becomes the site of the life-giving time" (5:16). (Rather than attempting to parse and explain this incredible passage, I will only suggest the reader spend some time with it.)

The importance of not-knowing-with-wings is seen here: "Hence, when the understanding consciousness comes to rest in what it does not know, it has reached its utmost. The demonstration that uses no words, the Dao that is not a dao—who 'understands' these things? If there is something that 'understands' them, it can be called the Heavenly Reservoir—poured into without ever getting full, ladled out without ever running out, ever not-knowing its own source" (2:36; with some tweaking). Not-knowing is Openness.

This is being self-so; letting oneself happen, and in that letting, letting all things happen in others as in oneself. Thus, we see that it is not really about a cosmological explanation of origins at all, but simply being ourselves.

VIII

In Guo Xiang, the cosmological concept of self-so—that Dao is literally nothing and not the Source, and that things are therefore self-arising, uncaused and non-dependent happenings—seems a bit absolutist in tone. For Zhuangzi, it is merely a phenomenological description of how things appear to be. Dao is only experienced as an absence—and this says nothing about its existence or non-existence. The psychological impact of both statements is nevertheless the same. We are "ever not-knowing its [life's] source". Zhuangzi's suggested response is that we release ourselves into this absence in openness and trust. And this amounts to simply releasing ourselves into the inexplicable upwelling that is Life as the life that we are.

Thus the cosmological, it turns out, is really no different than the existential—how we experience life. And thus Zhuangzi identifies a parallel phenomenon in ourselves—we are present to ourselves only as an absence. We search for a fixed-self, an immutable someone, but we cannot find it. We experience ourselves as a lack. And again, his suggested response is that we harmonize with our experience; that we release into our unfixed-ness. This is his no-self; not no self, but no-fixed-self.

Zhuangzi thinks that harmonizing with our experience leads to a happier life. That's the practicality of the concept of self-so.

I speak of "releasing" ourselves because there is an activity involved here, and it goes against our default response to our existential dangle, our sense of being ungrounded. We "take our minds as our teachers". We choose to pursue a Ground of Being—a purpose providing God (in a variety of forms—even atheistic ones)—rather than exploring the implications of our actual experience of ungroundedness. Or we speak of despair and the absurdity of existence upon our failure to find that Ground—because we never left the rationalistic pursuit at all.

Self-so-ness in us implies freedom to choose. Zhuangzi suggests we choose the "obvious". And this means harmonizing with life as it manifests, not as we wish it to be. But this in itself is not his chief value; his value is the enjoyment of life.

Though this philosophy is in some sense universally applicable, it is also the case that its value is contingent on perceived need. Those that find their solace in belief—or despair—are best left to enjoy the same. No need for salvation was ever implied. All is well in the Great Mess.

WANDERING
I - V

I

Wandering is Zhuangzi's paramount metaphor for the freedom of the sage. The image is so packed with suggested meanings that it is difficult to know where to begin.

Let us begin then with the most mundane—that it *is* mundane. Comparison with however we might imagine "enlightenment" suffices to demonstrate this. When it comes to so-called spiritual awakening, Zhuangzi seems to have set his sights relatively low. This, of course, is because the entirety of his project turns on his commitment to responding to life as it presents, not as we might wish it to be. This is summed up in the exhortation: "Add nothing to the process of life."

Wandering then takes place in this world and within the givens of our experience. No extra-mundane realities are posited or required.

There's something liberating in this alone. An imagined "enlightenment", the realization of some incredible *state* of being, is an invitation to mount a treadmill of perpetual aspiration and self-denial. Zhuangzi's wandering seems to be saying, forget all that; just enjoy yourself in the moment, just as you are.

Since we are typically attached and fixed to some one place, some merely "temporary lodging" that we insist on calling home, there is also work to be done here too, of course. However, since there's no fixed *state* to achieve, nowhere else we need to go, wandering, as merely an attitude, a psychological orientation, is always ready at hand.

Wandering requires no change, because everything is an occasion for wandering.

II

"Zhuangzi said, 'If a man has the capacity to wander, can anything keep him from wandering?'" (26; p 113)

Whether Zhuangzi actually said this or not, this statement speaks to the heart of what it is to wander.

Nothing can keep the wanderer from wandering because wandering depends on nothing. Indeed, wandering is precisely this non-dependence.

It follows that if we cannot wander in everything, then we cannot wander in anything.

We might think we are wandering in the "beneficial", but if we could not do the same in the "harmful", then we would not be wandering. Wandering is the transcendence of dependence on "benefit and harm".

This invites our imaginative meditation—further words are unnecessary; but here are some more:

"Let your mind be carried along by things so that your mind wanders freely. Hand it all over to the unavoidable so as to nourish what is central within you." (4:16)

"You just release the mind to play in the harmony of all *de*. Seeing what is one and the same to all things, nothing is ever felt to be lost." (5:6)

In non-dependence, nothing *can* be lost. There is nothing to lose.

III

If we have the capacity to wander, we can wander in all circumstances. But what is the "capacity to wander" and how do we get it?

Since I don't have that capacity, how could I say? Well, the saying is relatively easy, because the concept is easy. It is also the case that, as was likely with Zhuangzi himself, our interface with this possibility is dialectical. This is to say that it is "realized" only as and by approximation. Were it otherwise, if there was some final *state* that had to be achieved, then our wandering would depend on that and no wandering would be possible.

We can, therefore, wander in our inability to wander, or in our inability to wander in our inability to wander, or... If this doesn't seem to logically cohere, it is because it reflects the process of life itself. Does life make sense?

There seems to be two strains of methodology presented in the Inner Chapters. One suggests that we just take the leap, make the choice, just do it. "Hand it all over to the unavoidable."

The other suggests some form of meditation that brings us to the point where the wandering follows as a matter of course. The story in which Confucius begs to be the disciple of his disciple who has realized this serves as a case in point.

After much "sitting and forgetting" Yan has become "one with the Transforming Openness." "The same as it?" Confucius exclaims.

"But then you are free of all preference! Transforming? But then you are free of all constancy!" (6:54-5)

There is no reason why we cannot utilize both methods. Indeed, the practice of the one without the other might be impossible. This is especially the case when taking meditation as an imaginative excursion (as I do). We can only "hand it all over to the unavoidable" when we have imagined a point of view that encourages us to do so.

IV

Having become "one with the Transforming Openness", Yan is "free of all constancy". This is a delightful overturning of conventional value. Typically, to be constant is to be real. Transience is a lesser mode of being. (Essence precedes existence.)

To be constant is to be fixed; but to be fixed is to be incapable of wandering.

If we imagine reality as a Transforming Openness—an interpretive possibility which seems most consistent with our experience—then belief in anything fixed is delusory in any case. Since it is our psychological experience that most concerns Zhuangzi, it is the overturning of our sense of being a fixed-self that is at issue here.

This same Yan is he who discovered his core emptiness and thus realized that he "had yet to begin to exist". He realized no-fixed-self—a self-experience in which one's identity becomes merely a "temporary lodging".

"Seeing all lodging places as one, let yourself be lodged in whichever cannot be avoided." Or, "Making your real home in oneness, let yourself be temporarily lodged in whatever cannot be avoided." (4:10; note 6)

The capacity to wander thus entails the loss of one's "me"—a fixed somebody that fears the loss of its own self and cannot therefore escape the tyranny of "benefit and harm".

Perhaps this is why Zhuangzi lit upon "wandering" as his chief metaphor for freedom. The wanderer has no other home than the world itself. She has hid her self in the world—"hid the world in the world where nothing can be lost."

The sage makes the Transforming Openness her home and can freely wander everywhere within it.

V

"Far-flung and unfettered" are two adjectives Zhuangzi uses to describe wandering. They are mutually implying.

The first speaks to the boundlessness of the experience. Wandering is an excursion into vastness, limitlessness, emptiness, The Great Openness. These are "our homeland of not even anything" because they do not signify a *something* but merely a quality of experience. Openness is openness only when it remains open-ended, and that is possible only when it ultimately designates nothing in particular.

The second speaks to the quality of unfixedness so central to Zhuangzi's vision of freedom. Most important is the experience of no-fixed-self. One identifies with Transformation rather than one's immediate self-experience. One's present self-identity becomes a lightly held moment in time to pleasurably enjoy the mysterious Totality.

This core unfixedness affects our interface with everything else. We are no longer bound by fixed truths—nothing has to be true for us to be able to wander. We are no longer bound by the hopes and fears associated with "benefit and harm", but equally wander in whatever transpires. Life and death become a single string when there is no fixed-self to lose.

These are framed in negation, though they are actually all about affirmation. It's all good. All is well. We might then also mention that to wander is to play, and that implies being playful. And that implies having a self that playfully plays. And this equates to the enjoyment of life—nothing more.

All this is just an imaginative exercise, needless to say. None of it is true. It's just a wandering.

THE NUMINOUS RESERVOIR
I – VII

I

The term "heavenly reservoir" (*tianfu*) and its apparent synonym "numinous reservoir" (*lingfu*) appear once each in the Inner Chapters. There is also mention of a "numinous platform" (*lingtai*) in the Zhuangzian-ly sympathetic 19th and 23rd chapters, which I will not consider here. This series will consider just what these terms might mean.

In this post I will look at the broader meaning of the terms and in subsequent posts I'll parse out its various implications. So as to provide context, I offer one passage here:

"Hence, when the understanding consciousness comes to rest in what it does not know, it has reached its utmost. The demonstration that uses no words, the Dao that is not a dao—who 'understands' these things? If there is someone who is able to understand them [in this sense], it can be called the Heavenly Reservoir—poured into without ever getting full, ladled out without ever running out, ever not-knowing its own source. This is called the Shadowy Splendor." (2:36-7)

Ziporyn takes this term to denote "the ideal state of mind of the Zhuangzian person", a "Daoist subjectivity" (p.37), and his translation attempts to establish this. I have taken it as referring to something a bit more organic, namely that "place" of the upwelling of life within us—that place where we experience ourselves as self-so—the "unthinking parts of ourselves". I may be mistaken, and it may be that it comes to the same thing in any case, since this too is about our psychological interface with this inexplicable self-so happening—ourselves.

What Ziporyn dismisses is the common belief that this Heavenly Reservoir refers to "the Dao that is not a dao". There is a similar metaphor in the *Laozi* that speaks of Dao as just such a limitless reservoir (4). But, unlike Laozi (apparently), Zhuangzi does not believe in "the Dao" and does not entertain ideas of communing with Dao. It thus more likely refers to the mind of the sage, a mind that is open to Happening where no specific happening is required.

This is the Shadowy Splendor—really great stuff that is no stuff at all—a wonderful self-so experience without apparent cause or reason. It's like a fireworks display—bang, wow, gone. Why does that bother us?

II

I have essentially agreed with Ziporyn that Zhuangzi's Numinous Reservoir refers to the mind of the sage. It is openness to the whole of the life experience as it upwells within us. Openness amounts to complete affirmation of life just as it arrives. The passage previously quoted tells us that it is consequent to allowing the reasoning mind to come to rest in what it does not know. We can then be the unmediated experience that we are. This is the full extent of Zhuangzian mysticism. We don't ask and worry about the why of it; we simply enjoy it. In my (approximating) experience, thankfulness is an essential part of this enjoyment.

It is "numinous" (spiritual, mysterious) because it just happens—it is not experienced as made-to-happen by us or any known "Source". But this is not to say that it is anything other than the entirely natural. Mystery is what the reasoning mind cannot penetrate, and that is quite simply everything. There is no special something that is numinous—everything is numinous and invites our unmediated enjoyment.

There is that "place" in us, however, that is our most immediate experience of the numinous happening we call ourselves. It is simply the experience of self-arising, self-aware existence. If the mind of the sage is different than our own, it is in how it interfaces with this experience. There's nothing in the sage that is different from what is in all of us. The sage does not have more *qi* or extra-mundane anything than we do. She simply has a different *attitude* than we do. And attitude is as ephemeral as anything else. It changes nothing relative to ultimate outcomes; it just makes for a happier existence.

This, at any rate, is how I understand Zhuangzi's vision. This is not a religion. It's a philosophy of life.

Since we all share this experience of self-awareness, we can all explore how it manifests in us and how we relate to it. Self is a relationship; we can work on that relationship. I'll explore some of what this means and involves in the next post.

III

Self is a relationship. This, at least, is how it presents without our presuming some essentialist explanation—a soul, a true nature, a universal I Am, etc. We commune with ourselves. A prerequisite for self-awareness is dualism. "I" have my counterpart that I call "me". Ziqi said he lost his "me". Did he cease to be a self? No, he continued to speak about himself and to explain his experience—he was still self-reflective. Yet he was now also able to experience a sense of oneness with all things—he was not only an utterly unique self-so tree, but also the forest. This is omnicentrism—everything is Everything by virtue of its being its unique and distinct self. Everything explains everything else.

If we imagine viewing ourselves in a mirror with another mirror behind us this might give a metaphorical sense of what this experience entails. The reflection continues into theoretical infinity, so we now see it in a broader context; we see it at work and realize something of its ephemeral nature. Ziqi tweaked and expanded his self-relationship; he did not eliminate it.

I have said that the Numinous Reservoir is the mind of the sage and this involves a relationship with her own self-arising. We all share this experience; what differs is the qualitative character of that relationship. It's a matter of attitude. Having released herself from the need to know the why or what of it, she can release herself into an unmediated experience of life. This is spontaneous living.

But spontaneity suggests acting without reflection. Is that even possible or, if so, desirable? I think not, and will speak to this next.

IV

From the fragments of his writings that have survived we understand that Shen Dao (395-315 BCE) was a Legalist (one whose pessimism about human nature led him to discard the idea of societal order through self-cultivation, and instead advocated for strong laws). As he is represented in the *Tianxia* ("The World under Heaven") chapter of the *Zhuangzi*, however, he sounds much more like a proto-Daoist. It is he that said, "Just become like an inanimate [unconscious] object... Indeed, a clump of soil never strays from the Dao" (33; p 122). This led his detractors to declare: "Shen Dao's dao is no practice for the living, but it is a perfect guideline for the dead!"

To my thinking, Shen Dao was on to something important, especially if we take his statement as speaking to ontological reality—it is impossible for *any*thing to stray from metaphysical Dao if Dao is whatever happens. With respect to the ideal of fully realizing spontaneity, on the other hand, his statement serves to illuminate a fundamental problem, namely, how we can act spontaneously while remaining self-reflective. We are told that Shen Dao "was like a twirl in the breeze, like a spinning feather"—he let himself go without reflection. This would indeed be a good dao for the dead.

(I cannot resist making mention here of the apparent belief that because Shen Dao advocated something, he actually realized it. When we see how ridiculous this is, we can bring that discernment to bear on every such advocacy. I certainly apply it to Zhuangzi. The religious mind hungers for a fixed ideal—"the way", the sage, the Buddha—so as to escape the inescapable unfixity of the human condition.)

This long-winded introduction is intended to make the case for an appreciation of the dialectical character of spontaneity. Even in spontaneity there is always self-awareness; we are not yet dead. The dialectical is non-linear; it is an organic process that does not lend itself to final and definitive statements. And it is applicable across the board—it speaks to every aspect of the project of self-cultivation. There is no arriving, only growing. There is no final realization, only approximation. If one were to stumble into buddhahood, it would be because one let go into the dialectical nature of the human experience.

V

I will finish this series with a consideration of a passage recently mentioned in the discussion of the opportunities for self-cultivation that the unavoidable circumstances of life provide. Zhuangzi has "Confucius" tell us that we need not allow these circumstances to enter our "Numinous Reservoir", and then tell us what this means for our experience:

"That is what allows the joy of its harmony to open into all things without losing its fullness, what keeps it flowing on day and night without cease, taking part everywhere as the springtime of each being. Connecting up with This, your mind becomes the site of the life-giving time. This is what it means to keep the innate powers whole" (5:16-17).

This amazing passage seems to promise an experience of the celebration of Life itself in opening up to the "life" found in all happenings (things and events). This is an exciting prospect, and well worth pursuing. But let us begin by sobering ourselves up a bit. The passage is obscure and difficult to translate. This may not be what Zhuangzi had in mind at all. So what? Is this scripture? Is Zhuangzi's intended meaning the truth of things? Did Zhuangzi actually experience it, and if so, in what sense? Could we possibly experience it even if it is not what he had in mind?

All these questions are important principally because they serve to shift our relational focus away from belief and toward open-minded, imaginative exploration. "Release the mind to play." It's all psychological. It's all about how we can experience life, not what life and reality really, really are.

I am not a "follower" of Zhuangzi. I find his philosophy an incredibly insightful and inspiring point of departure for my own exploration of the possibilities for enjoyment that life provides me. And in the end, it is the exploration itself which must be that enjoyment, irrespective of any imagined discoveries or destination. It's all about the journey; the final destination is unavoidable however we get there.

VI

"That is what allows the joy of its harmony to open into all things without losing its fullness, what keeps it flowing on day and night without cease, taking part everywhere as the springtime of each being. Connecting up with This, your mind becomes the site of the life-giving time. This is what it means to keep the innate powers whole" (5:16-17).

"That is ... ." What is? Not allowing the vicissitudes of life to enter your Numinous Reservoir in such a way as to disturb your peace. All that happens is embraceable, because the Totality is ultimately affirmable. (All is well in the Great Mess.) In this way, one is in harmony with oneself and the world, and this makes for joy. Joy is something worth having. And this joy in utterly non-contingent—it depends of nothing. It is life allowed to be itself. It is not happiness as mutually arising with its opposite unhappiness, but a kind of non-happy happiness.

Not discriminating between events as affirmable or unaffirmable carries over into a sense of unity with "all things", an experience of the loss of one's "me" as the transcendence of the I/other dichotomy. It allows one to "open into all things". Guo Xiang calls it "vanishing into things".

Yet this vanishing into unity does not mean the loss of one's own special self-ness, one's "fullness". This suggests Ziporyn's "omnicentrism", a difficult concept, yet a potentially mind-expanding one. The Totality is not the center, an exclusive center that would negate differences. Things do not have their value by virtue of their being part of the "One", but the "One" has its value by virtue of the many. Every individual thing is the center, a non-exclusive center. Every individual thing is and explains Everything. It's infinite worm-holes into Unity.

This has practical implications in that one realizes the greatest unity with the world through realizing the cultivation of one's own uniqueness as the gate into that unity. And this holds true for everyone else, as well. Differences are respected and honored.

These are a few brief personal reflections on this passage. I'll conclude in the next post.

VII

"That is what allows the joy of its harmony to open into all things without losing its fullness, what keeps it flowing on day and night without cease, taking part everywhere as the springtime of each being. Connecting up with This, your mind becomes the site of the life-giving time. This is what it means to keep the innate powers whole" (5:16-17).

What this passage appears to be telling us is that the celebration of one's one unique life experience can become a celebration of all life (and being) experiences. In fact, the more one enjoys one's own self-arising, the more one is able to participate in the joy of every self-arising. We doubtless are immediately concerned that this is some form of egoism, but it is quite the opposite in that our openness to ("opening into") whatever happens also enables our opening into all others.

Ziporyn capitalizes "This" (*shi*) so as to link it with its technical usage in the Second Chapter where "this" and "that", the opposites of subjectivity and objectivity (self/other) and the moral discriminations (right/wrong) that arise from this fundamental dualism, are understood as susceptible to being united to form a oneness. This unity is "This", the totality of experience including the "something" that is always left out. Embracing the whole of experience enables one's mind to become "the site of the life-giving time". In this sense, the Numinous Reservoir is a shared experience. All things are happening together in one great riot of joyous self-arising.

This again brings us back to the logically irreconcilable mutual validity of the One and the Many that omnicentrism suggests.

This passage is an important one because it puts some very specific flesh on the bones of Zhuangzi's vision of sagacity. Since this is a purely psychological affair, its "truthfulness" lies entirely in the possibility of its being experienced. And that can only be determined when one commits to seeing if it can. But since it remains in the sphere of exploration, it need not require a commitment of belief or hopeful expectation. The advantage of looking for a pot of gold on the other side of the mountain is not in finding it, but in discovering what is actually there.

RELIGIOUS-MINDEDNESS
I – II

I

Anyone acquainted with my writing will know that I have an issue with what I call religious-mindedness. This is not so much directed at religion *per se* as it is toward what purports to be non-religious and yet is. Dogmatic atheism is as religiously-minded as any religion. Rationalism is religiously-minded. And most New Age philosophizing is utterly steeped in it.

Before exploring what this means and why I find it counter-productive, it would probably be best to mention one reason why it is likely so important to me. I once became a born-again Christian. Though admittedly assisted by LSD, the experience so deeply affected me that it took many years to wear off. When it did, I was pretty much inoculated against any further outbreaks.

I hope the reader will forgive me this biographical note; but doing this kind of philosophy necessarily has a personal context, some of which needs sharing. It is intended to provide the reader with that "grain of salt" that evinces the relative character of what is said here. In a word, it helps us both avoid: religious-mindedness.

Identifying the personal nature of this perspective also serves as an opportunity to make clear that this is not about the right dao versus a wrong dao. What works best for the individual is that person's right dao. Some do well in belief; others cannot believe. This dao is for one (me) who can't believe and who requires a different strategy by which to address our inherent need for a guiding dao. And needless to say, at best it can only provide some raw materials for the evolution of other daos just as it is itself so evolving.

"Daos are made by walking them", says Zhuangzi. And there are as many daos as there are pairs of feet to walk them. "Truth", opines Kierkegaard, "is subjectivity." It ultimately comes by way of *choice*, not objective certainty.

II

Religious-mindedness is essentially uncritical belief. It is an un-self-aware flight from our actual existential, human experience. It is in this sense inauthentic—it does not live life as it actually presents, but as it wishes it to be. There can be authenticity in belief, but it requires the honesty that also embraces the accompanying doubt. Since doubt is usually taken as the contradiction of belief, however, this is not the kind of belief typically espoused. The consequence is inner conflict and denial.

We all have our beliefs, needless to say. Most of these more closely resemble "trust". We believe it is worthwhile getting out of bed in the morning and to get on with the business of living. Though we likely do not first contemplate our reasons for doing so, we likely have some fundamental sense that it is. This is life being and doing itself—living. Trust is living. Living is trust. Ultimately, there is no *raison d'etre*—no reason to be—other than the apparent fact that we are. Belief is adding to life; trust is living it.

Any belief in fixed, objective "truth" is religious-mindedness. This statement must therefore also be religiously-minded—unless it can be upayic—unless it can self-efface and allow a return to doubt.

The surest sign of religious-mindedness is closed-mindedness; they are essentially the same. Open-mindedness is the opposite of religious-mindedness and its cure. Radical open-mindedness describes the essential mystical experience advocated by Zhuangzi and most other philosophies of his stripe. Another name for it is "emptiness". Emptiness is release from everything grasped and into

271

all things. Emptiness is release into vastness, which is the fullness of all things because it does not cling to any one thing. This enables Zhuangzi's "soaring".

If religious-mindedness and open-mindedness are opposites, can they not be "united to form a oneness"? Of course. This is open-mindedness. Open-mindedness in the real world is just this dialectic—a perpetual process of self-effacement by way of inclusion. Belief in the hypothetical sage who requires no such dialectic can easily lead us into religious-mindedness. For this reason we are entreated to discard the sages and worthies. If they exist, just let them be.

Get real. Be real. Be honest.

This blog is steeped in religious-mindedness. This entire project has its religious aspect. And the only "cure" is for me to admit it and to unite it with its opposite so as to form a oneness. This is realizing open-mindedness—approximatingly so. Failing of that, I can unite with that... and that...

THE EMPTY CENTER
I – V

I

The heart of philosophical Daoism is its acknowledgement and embrace of the empty center. The classic articulation is found in *Laozi* 11: "Thirty spokes make a wheel, but it is the empty center that makes it useful." There is really no thing or concept that does not participate in this core emptiness. Daoism, therefore, seeks to make the best possible use of it. This is Zhuangzi's "usefulness of the useless."

If we could fill that emptiness, attempting to do so would be a worthy project. The underlying premise of Daoism, however, is that we cannot. That attempt would thus be a futile activity, and one that alienated us from our most essential experience. Zhuangzian Daoism is all about engaging with our actual experience so as to see how we might make the life experience as enjoyable as possible. It is not a flight from reality, but a flight through it.

For self-aware human beings this emptiness is omnipresent. This does not mean that it "exists", but only that for beings that think of existence and non-existence it is unavoidable. It is a purely human phenomenon, and there is really no justification for objectively projecting it onto Reality and making it descriptive of the cosmos. Emptiness is, in this sense, just another empty concept. It is empty of itself.

II

On the epistemological level the omnipresence of emptiness is a consequence of our absolute cluelessness. We haven't a clue. There may very well be purpose, meaning, Truth, but the only ones we "know" are the ones we make up. On the ontological level, which is to say what we "feel" consequent to how we actually are in the world, these things naturally arise, though they cannot be rationally justified. Zhuangzi suggests we affirm and embrace this latter, though never to the point of knowing the truth of it. It's a matter of trust. Entrust yourself to life. Entrusting oneself to life is no different than entrusting oneself to the Great Happening. They are the same.

Still, we are rational beings and the exercise of reason is as much a part of being human as anything else. Only when we do so, we are confronted with an omnipresent emptiness. All understanding is ultimately groundless.

If this is a problem, it is also an opportunity. It is our not-knowing that occasions our surrender in trust.

If we knew our Source, we would be well-grounded. But this "Source" is really only present as an absence. It seems "necessary", but maybe it's not. Maybe Guo Xiang was right and everything is self-so, spontaneously self-arising, without cause. "The Source" too is an empty concept.

Much of Daoism and most of its interpreters like to make Dao the Source. There's lots of textual justification for doing so. Even Zhuangzi seems to dance around and flirt with the possibility. However, when we take Zhuangzi as consistent, we see that these flirtations, like his use of reasoned argument, are for the purpose of their own self-effacement. Whether there is a Source or not is immaterial in the face of our persistent not-knowing.

Nor, for Zhuangzi, is Dao a something with which we can unite or commune. Attaining Dao is a psychological experience, nothing more. Again, this is simply taking the fundamental sense of emptiness seriously and consistently.

Our hunger for grounding, our desire to fill the emptiness, is so strong that even those philosophies that make much of emptiness must constantly battle to remain true to this experience. They mostly fail.

III

Artists are often those who take the lead in addressing our essential sense of emptiness. The existentialist novel, Dada, surrealism, absurdism, and 'pataphysics come to mind. It was in reflecting on the tentative definition of this latter that led me to this reconsideration of the empty center. That definition reads "the science of imaginary solutions and the laws that govern exceptions".

This definition invites us to enter a realm of thought where there seems to be some sense in it, though none can really be found. It pulls us out of out of our knowing and into a sense of unknowable possibility. For the artist, this is the creative edge.

What it really comes down to is openness. Emptiness is the experience of a lack; but it is also an opportunity to expand and dissolve into the imaginary. Guo Xiang (252-312) speaks of "vanishingly uniting" with all things, and I think this is what he meant. His philosophy is very cerebral, but I suspect he also experienced something of which he wrote.

This imaginary movement has its focus on the Totality, but that has no real conceptual form. Openness is not so much openness *to* something as it is simply being open. It is, in effect, emptiness.

Emptiness is an experience. A human experience. It is not nothingness—who or what in nothingness could experience nothingness? Emptiness is self-awareness being its own lack. And this entails not the diminishment of the self-experience, but its infinite expansion. Only now it is not so insular—or fragile. Now it is not so completely identity-bound, but can be any identity without loss.

IV

Emptiness has its beginning and end in the most fundamental human experience. It is the third term where self-consciousness is necessarily dual. What lies between "I" and "me"? Emptiness. Human self-consciousness comes at a price, and this is it.

In the "fasting of the heart/mind" passage of the *Zhuangzi* the whole point seems to be the rediscovery of this emptiness. See with *qi* (*ch'i*), Confucius tells his disciple Yan. What is *qi*? "But the vital essence [*qi*] is an emptiness waiting for [*dai*, depending on] the presence of beings. The Dao alone is what gathers in this emptiness. And it is this emptiness that is the fasting of the heart" (4:9).

When Yan gives this fasting a try he discovers what this emptiness really means. "Before I find what moves me into activity, it is myself that is full and real. But as soon as I find what moves me, it turns out that 'myself' has never begun to exist. Is this what you mean by being empty" (4:10)? "Exactly", replies Confucius.

What moves him into activity is the emptiness that creates a space for him to fill. But then it is not "he" that is the real activator, but emptiness. His sense of being a concrete self, it turns out, is only imagined. Self there is, only now it is unfixed, fluid, transitory, and negotiable. Now, any self will do. "Sometimes he thinks he's a horse, sometimes he thinks he's an ox. Such understanding is truly reliable, such *de* is deeply genuine" (7:1). When Zhuangzi says, "Just be empty, nothing more" (7:13), this is what he means—have no-fixed-self. In this way we can wander in all things.

Still, emptiness "depends on" the presence of beings. Emptiness is not something out there that pre-exists things; it "exists" only because there are things. Or more specifically, only because there is a human being whose self-consciousness creates the occasion for emptiness to arise.

As always, this is all about the human experience. It is not a metaphysical theory of the nature of Reality. This too is being empty.

"Dao alone gathers in this emptiness." The experience of Dao is the experience of this emptiness—an emptiness that is populated by all things, a vastness—"the vastest arrangement".

V

Self-consciousness requires a gap, and that gap means we are never quite "full and real". This is our empty center, the price we pay for self-awareness.

This is how we evolved. There's no need to get all metaphysical about it. We needn't posit a great "fall" from some previously pristine state to which we must now struggle to return. This is how we are. There is no reason to project emptiness onto Reality just because it happens to be our experience. We needn't declare Reality "Mind" just because we happen to have one. Our anthropocentric hubris knows no bounds. Even God exists because we need "him" to do so.

Zhuangzi utterly de-mythologizes humanity. He suggests we take a sober look at how we are not "special", but are rather completely equalized together with all things in this Great Happening. Though we might prefer to be "gods" ("a little below the angels", as the Bible has it), still there remains a path to comfort in the realization of our total participation in ceaseless Transformation (our identity included). Indeed, where being "special" can only be a tentative hope at best, one beset by doubt and the fear of loss, release into the whatever of reality is freedom from all loss.

It is very much a part of modern thinking that we are one with Nature, though residual essentialist yearnings still remain. The "scientific" mind holds this view. But Zhuangzi suggests something more—a mystical movement, a release into this Mystery. This is a mysticism without specific belief, without a metaphysics, but is rather simply the exercise of inherent trust.

A DAOIST EXISTENTIALISM
I – VII

I

The theme of this series is inspired in part by Robert Miller's *Buddhist Existentialism: From Anxiety to Authenticity and Freedom* to which I will make occasional reference.

This presentation of a form of existentialism that takes its inspiration from Daoist philosophy serves two purposes. First, it faithfully represents the actual philosophy that Zhuangzian Daoism especially has led me to embrace. It is not simply something conjured up, but rather something that has grown out of my engagement with both existentialism and Daoism. Secondly, it serves to further distance this philosophy from any presumption of representing itself as the "correct" interpretation of Zhuangzian Daoism.

This latter has become increasingly important to me for several reasons. Perhaps most importantly, it renders the philosophy consistent with what I take as fundamental to Zhuangzi, namely the inescapable ambiguity of every cognitive representation of reality. We must all of necessity have a point of view, yet every point of view is perspectivally derived and utterly tentative. The exercise of this philosophy is thus not a pursuit of the truth, but rather a pursuit of an effective strategy by which to best live in the absence of truth. This, of course, is also fundamental to existentialism.

There is also the sense of contentiousness that arises from criticism of the interpretative takes of others vis-à-vis my own. Declaring what Zhuangzi is about necessarily involves disagreeing with others, and these others are for the most part significantly more scholarly qualified to speak than I. Though such disagreements are unavoidable, an understanding of this philosophy as derivative, that is, as one that *makes use of* Zhuangzi rather than attempts to represent him, allows this disagreement to be other than about the truth of things.

All this was previously addressed in the series A New Philosophical Daoism. This series simply puts a finer edge on the character of that philosophy and casts it in a bit more secular light. In both, the use of the indefinite article "A" is important in that it indicates that it is but one among many possible daos.

II

Very much like Daoism itself, there are many voices within existentialism, and not all "existentialists" ever in fact identified as existentialist. The best known strain has its point of departure in phenomenology, beginning with Husserl, and preceding through Heidegger and Sartre. If I have not already turned you off, let me say here that my understanding of phenomenology is very simplistic and I have no intention of attempting to go beyond that. For me, phenomenology simple means the study of experience as it manifests without the imposition of preconceived ideas. It describes rather than explains. Our engagement with that experience is thus immediate and existential. We ask how we might best respond rather than how we can make sense of it.

A good example of how this works can be seen in our self-experience. Taken as actually experienced, no concrete entity, the "self", can be identified. It's all very fleeting and tentative. Zhuangzi explores this experience and attempts to align his actual living with it. Our more default response, on the other hand, is to posit some form of reified self, a soul or true self that relieves us of our fear of ambiguity and doubt and our own possible non-being.

This is where authenticity comes in. Which of these responses best reflects actual experience? Which one best enables us to live life as it actually manifests whatever difficulties that might ensue?

Zhuangzi's description of the actual human condition is phenomenological. "Worn and exhausted to the point of collapse, never knowing what it all amounts to—how can you not lament this?" (2:11) He sees this as somewhat unavoidable, but he also sees the artificial imposition of redemptive formulae as only adding more suffering. "If you regard what you have received as fully formed once and for all, unable to forget it, all the time it survives is just a vigil spent waiting for its end." Deeming our self as a real and concrete entity only serves to exacerbate our suffering. All Zhuangzi's philosophy is an attempt to avoid such idealistic fantasies in favor of harmonizing with our actual experience.

Authenticity, though it has its own special challenges, is preferable to inauthenticity in that it accommodates to life as it actually manifests and that leads to a happier experience. All this is predicated on the exercise of a critical self-awareness, however. Where that does not exist, as it presumably does not among non-human species, there is no need for it to be otherwise.

III

Robert Miller (*Buddhist Existentialism*) offers seven attributes of existentialism that he sees as compatible with Buddhist sympathies. The first of these is the orientation posited by Sartre that "existence precedes essence". Since Plato, who thought that everything is what it is by virtue of its participation in and reflection of an Ideal, essence has been taken as preceding existence, the merely accidental. Everything is anchored and secure in the Ideal, Truth, God. Even empirical science defines things on the basis of their participation in a generalized class. You are human because you belong to the species Homo sapiens, not because you make yourself human.

Turning this on its head and declaring that existence, our experience, is really all we know robs life of all presupposed meaning. If there is meaning, it is that which we make for ourselves. There is only this experience as a becoming, or as Zhuangzi would say, a ceaseless transforming. This amounts to the experience of emptiness. There is nothing there to grasp though there seems to be something there that wishes there was. It is also a kind of openness. It is not "I" that is open to things outside myself, but the "I" itself that is an openness. It is open in every direction and in every way. It's identity is unfixed.

There is freedom here. But freedom always has its price. It is dizzying. Scary. And it's likely not for everyone. If it were, we'd be back at declaring the essence of things—what we *should* do. Zhuangzi's sage chooses this freedom. "Thus, the Radiance of drift and doubt is the sage's only map." In this she wanders. She fully engages in the life experience just as it manifests, just as she likes.

IV

In his concluding chapter, Robert Miller (*Buddhist Existentialism*) makes reference to 'pataphysics, a largely literary movement that began in late Nineteenth Century France. I have only a superficial knowledge of 'pataphysics which, in any case, is essentially undefinable by design. (Where in the dictionary does one put a word that begins with an apostrophe?) For the moment it suffices to consider only one attempted definition: "a science of imaginary solutions and the laws governing exceptions."

Most pataphysicians are of artistic and literary bent and Zhuangzi would have been most comfortable among them. What they have in common is the equation of the serious with the humorous. Only in the voidance of the serious in humor can the serious reflect the actual condition of existence. Where no "true purpose", true self, or any other of the multitude of essentialist fantasies are recognized, life presents as an opportunity for make believe, for play.

Existentialism, in taking the raw experience of existence as its point of departure, puts the burden of becoming squarely on the shoulders of the individual. It is up to us to decide how our life might best be lived. In this, it too is "a science of imaginary solutions". And this is what I believe Zhuangzi was also about—suggesting we use the power of imagination to find a way of being in the world that is in harmony with both our experience and our natural élan for enjoyment. Yet this can only work when done in the humorous spirit of play.

Play is the act of taking things most seriously in the awareness that they are not serious at all. It is walking two roads at once. We play to win, but if winning is the only goal, we are not playing at all. Life lived as play is life lived as open and empty. Nothing is grasped as essential; no personal dao excludes the daos of others. We are all "exceptions".

V

The subtitle to Miller's *Buddhist Existentialism, From Anxiety to Authenticity and Freedom*, speaks to both the positive possibilities of such a synthesis and an inherent weakness within Buddhism that makes it especially difficult. The greatest weakness of this book, in my opinion, is that it fails to escape the essentially salvific intentions of Buddhism. We need to be saved and Buddhism will save us. Buddhism is "the cure" for the human condition which is not humanity as it really is, but is a deviation from "the original mind" and the "true self" It is a deviation from how it *should* be. This is essentialism, not existentialism.

Can there not be authenticity in anxiety? Authenticity is not the achievement of some ideal state of mind, but the open and honest embrace of ourselves as we actually are in this moment, however we are. It is existential honesty. Its opposite is "bad faith" (Sartre), a dishonesty that leads to a flight from ourselves, inner conflict and hypocrisy.

Zhuangzian Daoism, to my thinking, lends itself much more easily to an existentialist interpretation and practice. We do not seek to escape the admittedly troubling aspects of our human experience—chiefly our insatiable hunger for fixed and sure moorings—but instead make use of them. We soar upon our mess, not away from it. Without the mess there could be no soaring, just as Peng could not fly without the monsoonal winds. This is the usefulness of the useless.

Authenticity then is the self-aware honesty and self-acceptance that enables us to pass into immediate affirmation and thankfulness. We need not strive for some idealist perfection, because we are already perfect by virtue of our being perfectly who we are, just as we are. This is the freedom that is now, not the freedom that must be earned and will likely never come.

All is well in the Great Mess, and in all our little messes as well. Nothing is lost; nothing need be saved.

VI

When existence precedes essence nothing is prescribed, nothing is mandated. We are free to choose our own dao, our own response to life. This is why there is such diversity in existentialist expressions. Some of these have been decidedly negative. Life has no essential meaning, and since we naturally hunger for meaning, life is absurd. According to Camus, our most pressing question is, Why not commit suicide? But this, to my thinking, remains squarely within the rationalist mentality; because life does not make "sense", it fails of inherent value.

It was to precisely this that Zhuangzi sought to offer an alternative. Rather than "taking our mind as our teacher", he suggested, why not rather surrender into life as it manifests? Life wants to live and flourish. In the human case, it wants to enjoy itself. So, why not completely identify with this élan and be that flow of life?

Still, there remains Unamuno's "tragic sense of life". Suffering, death, and loss still loom large as very real experiences for self-aware beings. The Zhuangzian response is not to deny and repress them, but to acknowledge and make active use of them. Our release into the Great Happening is facilitated by our need to do so. "Handing it all over to the unavoidable" is an active reply to these very same vicissitudes. "Becoming one with Transformation" is a continual response to the fear of death.

The point is that a Zhuangzian existentialism is always engaged in these responses. Indeed, it *is* this engagement. We can imagine the hypothetical sage who has arrived beyond the need to so engage—

and Zhuangzi does—but to remain authentic and true to our own experience we must understand that the work we do now *is* our dao.

Zhuangzian existentialism is not the "cure" for our ailments; it is simply a means to make good use of them.

VII

Does existentialism allow for mysticism? It's been so long since I have read the work of existentialists that I can only say I have a vague memory that there are some who do. Kierkegaard's "leap of faith" could be taken as an invitation to mystical experience. But this, like every form of existentialist mysticism does not fall within the usual definitions of that term. Though Kierkegaard was a theist, no "leap" would have been necessary if he did not see the need to break through the threshold of rationalism, and the consequence of this leap is subjective, not objective truth.

Typically, mysticism is understood as some sort of union or communion with the Absolute. Existentialism knows of no such thing. Its mysticism must therefore be an opening up into not-knowing, into emptiness. This, in fact, is at the heart of Miller's case for a Buddhist existentialism. He explores the meaning and ramifications of *shunyata*, emptiness, and discovers that this is precisely what the skepticism of existentialism invites. There are no "answers"; there are no "cures". It's all Mystery. This is emptiness. No cognitive formulae are allowed here.

Emptiness is not just a description of how the "world" presents; it is also a practice. It is the continual act of voiding our tendency to make cognitive sense of things, to seek a firm and objective ground that affirms our hunger to be the same, fixed and sure. This activity is mysticism in that it is the abandonment of the knowing-mind in favor of release into Mystery. Mysticism entails *experiencing* "something", and that's what this activity enables.

This, at my reading, is precisely that for which Zhuangzi advocates. Release yourself into Mystery. Wander in not-knowing. Be how life is. Transient. Unfixed. Empty.

Though scholars and interpreters of Zhuangzi never tire of telling us that he advocated for "union with the Dao", nothing, in my opinion, could be further from the truth. This mostly comes from lumping him into a generalized understanding of "Daoism", and, quite frankly, an unwillingness to engage in the spirit of Zhuangzi himself.

VIII

My basic orientation has been existentialist for most my life. But existentialism does not itself provide a path to any particular purposeful trajectory in terms of what kind of life one wants to live. It is open-ended in this regard. This is its strength as well as its weakness.

For whatever reason—and there are no doubt reasons beyond my immediate control—my natural tendency is toward negation and pessimism. This is why Zhuangzian Daoism has proven to be such a good fit in terms of directing me in a more positive direction. I have chosen this "imaginary solution" as a path into a greater enjoyment of life.

This Daoist existentialism is by no means "the" dao, but simply the one that works for me. It is a chosen philosophy of life, where a multitude of such philosophies are equally valid. The real question is not which dao is "best", but which dao works best for you.

It seems clearly the case, that we are often stuck in a dao that does not in fact work best for us. We are typically born into a religion, certainly a culture, and just as certainly into a personal character. These bonds are not easy to break; nor should we expect that we will feel the need to do so, or could if we wished. It likely takes some kind of existential trauma for us to realize a genuine paradigm shift, a new dao, and that, unfortunately, will not necessarily be a more helpful dao. The loss of faith, for instance can be a gateway to freedom, or it can be a descent into cynicism and despair.

To my thinking, the attainment of some degree of existential freedom—free-thinking—is worth both the birth trauma and the subsequent adriftedness. It is not, however, something that we need prescribe for others—all things being equal in the vastest arrangement, in any case.

CHAOS LIVES
I – VI

I

This series is inspired in part by my recent reading of N. J. Girardot's *Myth and Meaning in Early Taoism* in terms of both agreement and disagreement.

The death of Chaos (*hun-dun*) is related in the closing story of the Inner Chapters:

The Emperors of the North and South would often meet in the Kingdom of the Emperor of the Middle whose name was Chaos. Chaos showed them such hospitality that these two decided to repay him for his virtue (*de*). "'All men have seven holes in them, by which they see, hear, eat, and breathe,' they said. 'But this one has none. Let's drill him some.' So each day they drilled him another hole. After seven days Chaos was dead" (7:15).

Though Zhuangzi is here making use of ancient folk lore, we have to be careful not to interpret him strictly on the basis of past meanings. He frequently takes the conventional and turns it to his own purposes, whether it be cosmology (*qi*, yin-yang) or personages (Confucius, Laozi, the madman Jieyu).

Chaos is *hun-dun*, a well-known mythological figure, found in many guises, usually faceless and sometimes anus-less. It represents the cosmos before there was differentiation and things. For Confucians the term was largely negative, representing the disorder present before the advent of (Chinese) civilization. The barbarian tribes represent chaos. For the Daoists it has a decidedly positive connotation in that it represents the ever-present "something left out that is the most important thing of all." In this contrast alone we see

SCOTT P. BRADLEY

the radical departure of Daoism from the conventional anthropocentric preoccupation with human yang-ing. Daoism suggests that our yang-ing, though necessary and affirmable, also does us (and the environment) harm when not placed in the context of yin, chaos.

Daoism emphasizes yin, not because it is "better" than yang, but because in our single-minded pursuit of knowledge and progress we have forgotten the equalizing valuation of yin wherein all things are affirmable just as they are. Yang informed by yin is yang off the debilitating treadmill of wanting to be other than we are.

This, in any case, is one slice of it.

II

Girardot would make Zhuangzi's story of the death of Chaos a direct representation of the creation myth from which Zhuangzi borrows. This fails for a number of reasons, not the least of which being that Zhuangzi sees this death as a negative event, not a positive one. The outcome is not the creation of the many, as in the creation myth, but simply the death of that which possibly precedes this event. It is, in any case, only a hypothetical within a myth; it does not represent any actual event, but seeks to make a statement about the nature of Chaos and our human propensity to deny it or attempt to eliminate it.

We need not fear for Chaos in any event. Chaos lives! Or more accurately, that which has never lived or existed can never die.

What then is Chaos? It likely does have some cosmological meaning as that which precedes the creation of the many. But like Dao, Zhuangzi is not really that interested in pursuing its metaphysical reality. It is only suggested by its seeming necessity, but in the end is present only as an absence. This is the essential attribute of Chaos; to know it is to kill it.

Zhuangzi is more interested in the epistemological presence of Chaos. Whenever we know something we draw a circle around it. But what lies outside this circle? Whatever it is—and there will always be something no matter how supposedly vast our circle—and it matters not at all what it is—it is more important to our understanding than that which we think we know. And this is because it tells us that we do not in fact know at all.

SCOTT P. BRADLEY

Chaos, the unknown and undifferentiated, or as I like to call it, Mystery, is the ever-present background that surrounds our personal little circles. It is an unavoidable fact of our experience. As such, to deny it or to vainly attempt to eliminate it by knowing it—to kill it—is to sever ourselves from what amounts to the most important aspect of our experience. And this is the death of our own Chaos; for we are indeed also Chaos. Where in Chaos can Chaos be lost?

Again, Chaos, the thing left out, is the "most important thing of all" only because it is left out. Non-existence is only more important than existence when it is forgotten. Death is only more important than life when it is denied. But it is only because life is so precious that death becomes so important. Life and death form a single string; they are equally "good" and affirmable. The point is to live in the context of both, which is to say, to live authentically.

III

The "seven holes" of the human face are the principle means by which we perceive the world. But to perceive the world is to become dual. When Chaos, which is non-dual, receives these holes, it dies; it too becomes dual.

Similarly, when we attempt to understand or perceive Chaos, we kill it. This is why these posts so militantly attempt to defend the inviolable impenetrableness of Mystery. Its only usefulness is its continued uselessness.

This understanding is by no means unique to Zhuangzi; many religions and philosophies of "Eastern" stripe declare the same. Yet every one of them, including "Daoism", tends to gravitate toward some essentialist reification of Mystery. It exists and can be encountered and "attained". Dedicated non-dualists hold symposiums intended to demonstrate how modern science "proves" the validity of their claims. So great is our desire to escape drift and doubt. This too is the death of Chaos. Now it exists within the circle of human understanding.

The preservation of Chaos as impenetrable Mystery is by no means the negation of the dual. To be human is to be dualistic. So let's hear it for dualism. It's all equal and affirmable. But dualism is not without its problems. And though these cannot be eradicated, they can be ameliorated through open-minded and imaginative excursions into "the vast wilds of open nowhere", "our homeland of not even anything", which is to say Chaos left to be Chaos.

There is no escape from the human condition in philosophical Daoism. There is no cure; there are only palliatives to ease the time before our passing. To presume a cure would be to murder Chaos of which we too are a "part".

IV

We can only take an imaginary excursion into Chaos. What? There's a thing called Chaos? No, Chaos is a psychological experience. And that is only had imaginatively.

We typically find this troublesome. If an "imaginary solution" is the best we can do, that hardly seems like a solution at all. Well, it isn't. It's a coping strategy. Only religious belief can provide a solution.

Or death. Death likely cures all ills. Who can say? No one—which tends to suggest the point. But to seek it would be the "nuclear option", and can hardly be described as an authentic response to the élan of life which is to live. Best to "hand it all over to the inevitable" and to enjoy life as it is while it is.

But if taking an excursion into Chaos is only an exercise of the imagination, then many other strategies are also likely possible. Yes, I must admit that even my bête noire, religion, is such an imaginary strategy, though it does not know it. But knowing it makes all the difference when it comes to living authentically. Living authentically entails being real about our actual existential experience. And that is to live in "drift and doubt", to live our existential dangle.

I imagine there are other authentically self-aware imaginary excursions possible, but I can't say I can think of any. The thing about Chaos is that it is at the heart of our human experience. It is none other than our own empty center. Whatever other authentic strategies there might be must therefore be in response to this. Or so it seems to me.

V

The Emperors of the North and South both have names, Hu and Shu, and we would like that their meaning might add to our understanding of the passage. Despite Girardot's predictable attempts to make the connection, however, any possible allusion to mythological figures connected to a creation myth is tenuous at best. Both names suggest something like "hasty" or "sudden" and this is more suggestive of Zhuangzi's more immediate purpose than to illustrate the birth of the many.

Zhuangzi's attitude relative to the emergence of things is clearly seen in his ironic utilization of infinite regress to demonstrate that our speculations about the ultimate origins of the Universe are a waste of time. "There is a beginning. There is a not-yet-beginning-to-be-a-beginning. There is a not-yet-beginning-to-not-yet-beginning-to-be-a-beginning... Now I have said something. But I do not-yet know; has what I have said really said anything? Or has it not really said anything" (2:31)? The Big Bang is a possible beginning; but what is the not-yet-beginning-to-be-a-beginning?

His more immediate meaning in using names that imply hastiness is seen in the consequences of their precipitous actions. Seeking to repay Chaos for his virtue (*de*), they believed that *helping* him would be an exercise of *their* virtue. They killed him with kindness. They felt more "virtuous", but he was dead.

This speaks to that most important Daoist concept of *wu-wei*, not-doing. It is not that the desire to help others is mistaken, but that the means goes amiss. Taking coercive action—drilling him seven holes—is yang-ing, and does more harm than good. Being the empty space that occasions the movement toward change in another, on the other hand, is yin-ing. Yin-ing is non-being the change.

We see this in the Socratic Method in which Socrates does not contradict the opinions of others, but simply questions them so as to assist them to come to their own conclusions. We see it in Rogerian psychology wherein the client is assisted in discovering his or her own solutions. And, of course, we see this throughout the Inner Chapters in the irony of theses posed only to be deconstructed so as to leave us in ambiguity and doubt.

The Inner Chapters can, in fact, be taken as single koan designed to help us go where its yang-ing words cannot.

VI

Good intentions do not justify precipitous action. This is yang, self-assertiveness. Yin, on the other hand, is a passiveness that fulfills those intentions non-actively. It is a kind of midwifery—an encouraging presence that lets the other give birth to her own. It is the way of water—yielding, taking the lower ground, yet transforming all things. It is an essential quality of Dao.

So important is this to Zhuangzi's vision that he makes it an occasion for the birth of true friendship. Three friends "came together in friendship, saying, 'Who can be together in their not being together, do things for one another by not doing things for one another? Who can climb up upon the Heavens, roaming on the mists, twisting and turning round and round without limit, living their lives in mutual forgetfulness, never coming to an end'" (6:45)?

This is a third way, somewhere beyond intrusive self-assertion and indifference. These friends are together while they are not; help one another by not helping one another. Somehow this makes one think of love. True love holds so lightly that it hardly holds at all. It lets the other be. This too is the nature of Dao. "Dao does nothing, yet nothing is left undone." All things flourish because Dao leaves them alone to do so. All things are self-so—self-arising, self-flourishing. Love allows just this.

It is not incidental that this "mutual forgetfulness" is made synonymous with carefree wandering. One climbs *upon* the Heavens and roams *on* the mists through an affirming acceptance of things as they are. Without them there would be nothing upon which to soar.

Mutual forgetfulness is only possible because there is friendship. Non-dependence is only possible because of our total dependence.

MY DEATH IS GOOD
I – IV

I

Whatever our attitude regarding death, it is clearly an event of momentous significance for all of us who live. There may be some who are inclined to glibly dismiss its importance to our every waking moment; they are likely either sages or in denial. For the rest of us, it is a reality that begs our attention. What does it mean that we shall die? How does our impeding death impact our living?

The totality of Zhuangzi's philosophy can be seen as a response to death. If this makes it seem limited or parochial, so be it. His philosophy is all about the human experience, and the awareness of our death—indeed, the apparent death of all things, including those we love—stands out as the most immediately pressing.

Zhuangzi's understanding of the human condition and his remedial response turn on our awareness of death. Our existential dangle—our suspension in utter not-knowing—matters only because of death.

"If you regard what you have received as fully formed once and for all, unable to forget it, all the time it survives is just a vigil spent waiting for its end" (2:11). If we take ourselves as a fixed-identity, something we can lose, then our actual living is adversely affected.

"In the process, you grind and lacerate yourself against all the things around you." Fearful of loss, we become fearful of everything that might threaten us, even what seems to diminish our sense of self. Loss of face is taken as an incremental death. We die a death of a thousand cuts.

If this seems excessively gloomy, I can only reply that it also seems honest. It is, in any case, a necessary prelude to whatever remedial response we might imagine.

II

My death is good—at least in theory. The realization of such an agreement with this unavoidable reality of life would be the accomplishment of a sage. At best, I can only attempt to approximate it.

Meditation on this simple statement "my death is good" can be a powerful imaginative exercise. It opens us to the heart of Zhuangzi's vision of total affirmation of the life experience. There is a real sense in which his philosophy can be summed up in one word—Yes! (And this is always followed in my experience with—Thank you!—though I am not sure why.)

In the previous post I spoke of the importance of death for an appreciation of life to the point that it could have been taken as morbidity. Since it is an unavoidable fact of life, however, to ignore it amounts to denial; and denial can only be a phantom escape. It simply lurks deeper and more insidiously. Had we the choice, we'd likely choose not to die, but since we do not, death presents as a wonderful opportunity to get real about our human experience.

"The Great Clump burdens me with a physical form, labors me with life, rests me with death. So, it is precisely because I consider my life good that I consider my death good." (6:26) Taken as a single unit, life and death are both affirmable, should we wish to affirm either. And we do affirm life, if we are in harmony with life itself which is by its nature a spontaneous affirmation.

The affirmation of death is an affirmation of the Totality, and there can be no such affirmation without it. I call it The Great Mess in recognition of the difficulty we have in doing so, and declare that All Is Well, in recognition of the possibility of affirmingly "basking it all in the broad daylight of Heaven". These represent the Two Roads we must walk simultaneously.

III

One of four soon-to-be friends said, "Who can see nothingness as his own head, life as his own spine, and death as his own ass? Who knows the single body formed by life and death, existence and non-existence? I will be his friend!" (6:40) Own the whole ball of wax.

This imaginative exercise is simple enough. Indeed, there is really nothing that profound about Zhuangzi's vision at all. It's simply a chosen response to the raw human experience.

Addressing the bondage of "Confucius" to conventional thinking, "Laozi" asks, "Why don't you simply let him see life and death as a single string, acceptable and unacceptable as a single thread, thus releasing him from his fetters?" (5:13)

The point is to take one's mind beyond its insular focus on the immediate, purely human context, so as to realize its broader context. Zhuangzi calls this recontextualization "the vastest arrangement". It can only remain the vastest, however, when it is entirely open-ended. Imagine "limitlessness". Is it possible? It is, it seems, only if something new and different happens to the mind. And that's the ultimate point of the exercise.

There is, however, also a more immediate and mundane benefit. Taking life and death as a single string, one body, our attitude toward both life and death can be approximatingly transformed. "The proof that one is holding fast to the origin can be seen in true fearlessness." (5:10) It may be that we are unable to realize total release from the debilitating fear of death, but we can realize incremental freedom.

It is important to keep the ideal in mind, but never to the point of undermining the ultimate value of the real and immediate. We want to be able to walk these two roads at once.

WALKING TWO ROADS
I – V

I

There is hardly a post in which I do not mention "walking two roads" or feel I could do so. It so neatly conveys the paradoxical relationship between the "heavenly" and the human that obtains whenever we imagine humanity outside its immediate anthropocentric context. It enables us to be informed by a "higher" point of view without negating the more parochial human point of view. By it we can care without caring, hope without hoping, grieve without grieving, fear without fearing, and nourish life without fearing its loss.

Zhuangzi actually uses the term only once, and then somewhat differently, and in a more complicated sense. I have, therefore, adopted it more broadly to describe what is nevertheless an important part of his overall vision.

In the story called Three in the Morning (2:23-4) a monkey trainer tells his monkeys that he'll be giving them three nuts in the morning and four in the afternoon. The monkeys are outraged. Okay, says the trainer, I'll give you four in the morning and three in the afternoon. The monkeys are delighted.

Several conclusions are drawn from this simple story. The first is that, "This change in description and arrangement caused no loss ..." In the vastest arrangement, where all things are equalized, just as 3+4 is the same as 4+3, so also are all things.

But more germane to our current topic is this observation: "Thus, the sage uses various rights and wrongs to harmonize with others and yet remains at rest in the middle of Heaven the Potter's Wheel. This is called 'Walking Two Roads.'"

SCOTT P. BRADLEY

There is the human world of rights and wrongs and there is the higher perspective that understands their relative nature and ultimate dis-valuation; they too can be united to form a oneness.

The sage can live in, appreciate and make use of both points of view simultaneously.

II

The purpose of the story of the trainer and his monkeys, Zhuangzi tells us, is to illustrate the folly of trying to prove the oneness of things. "But to labor your spirit trying to make all things one, without realizing they are all the same [whether you do so or not], is called "Three in the Morning."" (2:23)

This is most likely a reference to Zhuangzi's sparring buddy Huizi who did precisely this. As a conclusion to his many paradoxes was the pronouncement: "Love all things without exception, for heaven and earth are one body." (33; p 124) Zhuangzi obviously does not disagree with the sentiment, but only with the means of realizing it. Indeed, he exclaims the same sense after his own series of paradoxes: "Heaven and earth are born together with me, and the ten thousand things and I are one." (2:32)

Some scholars take this to be an ironic dig at Huizi, that it does not actually express Zhuangzi's opinion. I disagree. The difference between the two is that for Huizi it was a logical conclusion and for Zhuangzi it was an ecstatic experience. If we apply his story of the monkeys here, we see that he does not disagree with the conclusion per se, but only that it never leaves the realm of reason. Huizi always and only took his mind as his teacher.

Huizi is likened to the monkeys, worrying himself about immediate differences without intuitively (phenomenologically) realizing that there is no need to do so. Zhuangzi, of course, is the monkey trainer, at least in his imagined scenario. He experiences the oneness of things such that he can walk two roads at once—he can flexibly

329

follow along with every parochial expression while never clinging to any one.

III

The question of the relationship between the "Heavenly" and the Human is an important one to early Daoist philosophy, and there are decidedly different takes on the issue. We might best begin by getting an idea of what Zhuangzi means by the term "Heavenly" since it carries a lot of culture baggage in our present context. For him it simply refers to the inescapably unknowable Mystery of origins and "purpose" that the human mind seems to require. Originally, the term had more theistic, or at least volitional implications, as it might for us today, but in Chinese thought it evolved toward a more Zhuangzian point of view, though his tended to the extreme end, namely that it is only present as an absence and without cognitive content.

Since for Zhuangzi the Heavenly is an entirely ambiguous concept the relationship between it and Humanity is similarly ambiguous. It is unknowable. Humanity is itself therefore unknowable. Humanity is as much mystery as Mystery.

The importance of this relationship is determined by our desire for guidance, a dao. Can Heaven guide us? In a radical departure from conventional thought, Chapter One of the *Laozi* declares that it cannot. Any dao that daos (guides) is not the authentic Dao. Yet daos unavoidably remain, and can be affirmed as necessary. They are themselves mystery (given their ultimate groundlessness) and can therefore be taken as "the same" as the Mysterious Dao.

For some this might have suggested the abandonment of the Heavenly (Dao) altogether, but for Daoism it means that we can only "understand" ourselves in the context of Mystery. This represents a momentous movement into the realm of ambiguity, of not-knowing, that Zhuangzi fully embraces and to and by which he makes a creative response. This is making the useless the most useful thing of all.

Walking Two Roads can be understood as the practical application of this relationship between the Heavenly and the Human. All that we do upon the human road is done in an awareness of the implications of the heavenly road, which he takes as equalizing in its indeterminacy.

IV

It is because there is no definitive boundary between the heavenly road and the human road that we are able to walk them both at once. What they have in common is ambiguity, and it is through this that both roads pass. Zhuangzi admits that it would be great if there was such knowledge, if Heaven could give us clear guidance (dao us), but he concludes that it cannot (6:1-5).

If Heaven could tell us the right thing to do, then our only responsibility would simply be to do it. This is the consolation of religion. The path is clear. Things are black and white, without too much of the fearsome ambiguity of grey.

If, on the other hand, Heaven is understood as a Chaos in which questions of right and wrong have no meaning, then we are required to figure things out for ourselves in awareness of our lack of sufficient knowledge to definitively do so. We are cast into a world of uncertainty and doubt. The world is all grey, and our humanly acts of distilling a black and white from it is revealed as relative to personal and cultural contexts.

Zhuangzi sees this as an opportunity. Though we are pretty much obliged to have opinions, we can also understand them as only that. This allows us to "follow along with" the opinions of others, even when they are likely to be considered more than that. We are freed in having no-fixed-opinions, and this leads to tolerance.

The ambiguity of Heaven informs our human quest for the unambiguous such that we recognize the ambiguous nature of our unambiguous opinions. We walk the latter in the light of the former.

Ethical questions naturally raise their angry heads when we relativize right and wrong in this way, but we'll have to leave them for another time.

V

Nothing of the human is negated with the relativizing introduction of a higher point of view despite the fact that that point of view reveals a sense in which all these human activities are nonsense if taken too seriously. This holds true in two senses.

Perhaps most importantly, nothing that happens is not the Great Happening. Whatever humans do is as affirmable as anything else. If we look again at Chapter One of the *Laozi* we see that though any spoken dao is not the ultimate Dao, every spoken dao is nonetheless an expression of Dao. "They are the same." It is not possible to "stray from the Dao". If there is straying, then that straying is Dao.

This is the principle behind my personal mantra: I am perfect by virtue of my being perfectly who I am. I could not be otherwise. Nothing more is required. All is well even in my own personal mess. There is a great deal to achieve in the cultivation of myself, but nothing has to be achieved. Total affirmation is unconditional. Realizing this fully would be my idea of enlightenment, if there is any such thing.

Secondly, what humans do is what humans are. There is no ideal humanity, but only the humanity that is. This is who we are. We are not "better than this". If we are a mess then it is presently our nature to be so. We love, we hate, we rejoice, we grieve, we do "good", we do "evil"; all these things are human qualities and understanding that sense in which they are the same and equal, does not eliminate them.

What the introduction of a higher road, the view from Dao, does is allow us to live out our humanity in greater self-awareness. And that awareness releases us from the burden of taking ourselves and our world so seriously that we cannot play and wander within them.

IV

Zhuangzi's "vastest arrangement" is realized by "hiding the world in the world", yet another imaginative exercise. "When the smaller is hidden in the larger, there remains someplace into which it can escape. But if you hide the world in the world, so there is nowhere for anything to escape to, this is an arrangement, the vastest arrangement, that can sustain all things." (6:28)

Essentially, Zhuangzi suggests we so completely identify with the Totality that there is no place left for us to be lost. This does not guarantee a continuity of individual identity, but then we have presumably simultaneously accepted that we have no-fixed-identity in any case.

Is it possible for there to be some form of continuity that does not entail a continuity of identity? If so, it would seem to be beyond the ability of the mind to fathom, for words imply identity. The world as it manifests is one of constant change, Transformation, and this, we must conclude, precludes the perpetuation of any identity.

There is the story of the ship Janus that had so many refits that every last bit of her was replaced; how then could she still be called the same ship Janus? What's in a name? It seems rather arbitrary.

On the question of what becomes of us at death Zhuangzi is essentially mute. It doesn't matter, if we have handed all over to the unavoidable. This seems like a very logical act when you think about it. It is very much like the Skeptic's *ataraxia*, a state of peace and tranquility consequent to resting in what we do not know and cannot change. To what extent this is for them a mystical experience I do not

337

know; it most definitely is for Zhuangzi. It is equivalent to wandering free and unfettered within the world with which we have identified.

ONE
I – V

I

Zhuangzi is big on oneness. A sense of the oneness of things is the experience of Dao. It is this that releases us to play among all things, unencumbered by the divisive fetters of discrimination. Where this is good and that is bad, this is beneficial and that is harmful, this is beautiful while that is ugly—where these are in play, we cannot.

Yet the spirit of play also requires that we not fetter ourselves to a fixed idea about oneness. The idea of One certainly suggests itself, but we have no business making sweeping statements regarding the ultimate nature of reality. Here again our inviolable not-knowing is the axis upon which our orientation to our human experience turns. This, too, is the usefulness of the useless.

For Zhuangzi, oneness is a beneficial psychological experience that requires no belief in metaphysical certitudes. Never do we leave the realm of ambiguity. Ambiguity is our freedom—should we wish to make it so. We wander when there is no particular place to go, and no need to go anywhere at all.

As a means to the experience of oneness Zhuangzi suggests an imaginative journey of perspective shifting: "Looked at from the point of view of their differences, even your own liver and gallbladder are as distant as Chu in the south and Yue in the north. But looked at from the point of view of their sameness, all things are one." (5:5)

Take your pick. Both perspectives are possible. Both are legitimate. Indeed, can we not experience and appreciate them both? Wouldn't this be walking two roads at once? In this way we can choose to experience a sense of oneness because it is *beneficial* without that involving us in a contradiction. Differences are as much a part of our human experience as sameness can be made to be.

I call this kind of movement imaginative meditation—not so much as to make it sound profound as to suggest that it is more than simply thinking about it. It is an exercise that can help us to actually experience something—something beneficial.

II

Looking at things from the point of view of their sameness is a relatively easy way to imagine the oneness of things. Zhuangzi's argument for "uniting opposites to form a oneness" is more complicated. This, in part, is because it is a step in a larger argument deconstructing the use of reason as a means to understanding ourselves in the world context.

Zhuangzi makes use of the terminology and techniques of the Mohists and Logicians to push their arguments beyond what they themselves had in mind. The former used logical argument to demonstrate what was "admissible" and what was not. This would lead to an understanding of how best to fulfill the first principle of their political strategy: love (care for) all things equally. There's some suggestion of Dao here, only its expression is not Dao in that it remains only conceptual and is actively applied. Love, in this instance, became tyrannical.

The Logicians used logic to demonstrate its internal contradictions through the use of the paradoxes that our discriminations about time, space and size naturally suggest. ("The south is both bounded and boundless, so you can go to Yue today and arrive yesterday.") (33; p 124) This led Huizi to exhort: "Love all things without exception, for heaven and earth are one body." (33; p 124) The breakdown of our ability to logically divide up the world, led him to a declaration of its unity.

For Zhuangzi, both made a good start, but failed to go far enough—they never left the realm of reason, "the understanding consciousness", but rather continued to "take their minds as their teacher". What's the alternative? A mystical re-integration with the life-experience.

It's curious how all three arrived at essentially the same conclusion. After a series of his own paradoxes, Zhuangzi declares: "Heaven and earth were born together with me, and the ten thousand things and I are one." (2:23) The difference is that for Zhuangzi this is an ecstatic *experience* while for the other two it remained an intellectual concept, something to apply to the world rather than something to be.

III

"This", a subjective point of view, creates "That", the view that it is not. "Self" creates "Other". Without the one there would not be the other. "This is the theory of the simultaneous generation of 'this' and 'that'." (2:16) But just as they create one another, so also do they destroy one another. Every "this" is also a "that", and every "that" is also a "this". Is there really then any "this" or "that"?

Whether there is or there is not, it is possible to "unite them to form a oneness". It is possible to imagine an experience in which all things "bask in the broad daylight if Heaven", an experience of the non-dual.

"When 'this' and 'that'—right and wrong—are no longer coupled as opposites—that is called the Dao as Axis, the axis of all daos." (2:17) Dao is the confluence of all daos—yours, mine, everyone's. Dao is the equalization of all theories about things and of things themselves, not because their sameness trumps their differences, but because we can imagine it thus.

This is the essence of Zhuangzi's argument in the second of the Inner Chapters. It's worth "trying on", he thinks, because it can transform how we relate to the world. It can issue in greater inner and outer peace.

"It is only someone who really gets all the way through them that can see how the two sides open into each other to form a oneness. Such a person would not define rightness in any one particular way but would instead entrust it to the everyday function [of each being]...

It's just a matter of going by the "rightness" of the present 'this'." (2:23) We might describe this as openness and tolerance.

The experience of the view from Dao enables an appreciation of all daos. It's a bit like an appreciation of Nature that allows for an appreciation of all its expressions—cobras as well as meerkats—deserts as well as forests.

This conceptual experiment is only a tool the intent of which is to bring us to the point of needing no such thing. "To do this without knowing it, and not because you have defined it as right, is called 'the Dao'." Imaginative exercises are just training wheels. But even these help us to go somewhere.

IV

The Daoist appreciation for Oneness does not diminish its appreciation of the many. Understanding things from the point of view of their sameness does not negate their differences. Indeed, we are invited to travel in both directions so far that they also are "united to form a oneness". The unconditional uniqueness of all things is their oneness. They are one and the same in being different.

This brings to mind Ziporyn's "omnicentrism" which he distills from Tiantai Buddhism as inspired by his reading of Zhuangzi. Every expression is the expression of all things. It is only in being themselves that things are all things. All things are the center; every expression expresses all things. There is no single Center; all things are the center.

The Daoist emphasis on Vastness in contrast to Emptiness also illustrates this sense. "The main principle of Buddhism is Emptiness: nothing is wanted; all is to be abandoned," wrote Liu Xianxin (1896-1932). "The main principle of Daoism is vastness: everything is wanted; all is to be included." (p 137) Whether this is a true representation of Buddhism or not, it does give a sense of the meaning of vastness. The "vastest arrangement" is that which includes all things as affirmed in their uniqueness, without diminishment.

When we identify with vastness, we are better able to let go of any one particular identity in realizing the unity of all identities without abolishing identity altogether. "You temporarily get involved in something or other and proceed to call it 'myself'... But when you rest securely in your place in the sequence, however things are arranged, and yet separate each passing transformation from the rest, then you enter the clear oneness of Heaven." (6:50-1)

Things are unavoidably "selves". The point is not to diminish self-ness, but to enjoy and be whatever self you might presently be without clinging to it in fear of its loss.

V

Speaking of the imaginary "ancients" Zhuangzi says, "Their oneness was the oneness, but their non-oneness was also the oneness. In their oneness they were followers of the Heavenly. In their non-oneness they were followers of the Human. This is what it is for neither the Heavenly nor the Human to win out over the other. And this is what I call being both Genuine and Human, a Genuine Human Being." (6:22-3)

This is walking two roads in a nutshell. Zhuangzi's sage is she who lives this paradox. To be genuine (authentic) is to make positive use of this inherent ambiguity. Zhuangzi began this passage by telling us that however great it would be to understand the boundary between these two roads, their relationship must remain forever unknowable. Oneness informs us in our non-oneness, but it does not diminish its affirmability.

Our non-oneness is also the oneness. Ultimately, there is no gap in reality. All is well. All is affirmable. Thus, I say, we are perfect by virtue of our being perfectly who we are, just as we are. If there is "enlightenment", this for me is its gate. If there is Buddha, then there is nothing that is not already Buddha. There is nothing to do; nothing to become; no conditions to meet; no salvation or redemption is necessary. It is all already totally affirmable. Rejoice and enjoy.

With this behind us, we can more effectively get on with the human non-oneness of improving ourselves and the world in which we live. There's lots to be done.

NON-BEING THE CHANGE
I – IV

I

In the Inner Chapters the celebrated fourth chapter passage recommending "fasting of the heart" has a practical emphasis that is often overlooked in our zeal to find a method for "spiritual enlightenment". The title of the chapter, "In the Human World", though likely an editorial add-on, should, however, alert us to its broader context. This, and other passages in this chapter, concern how to effect change in the political world.

Confucius' favorite disciple, Yan, wants to go to one of the "Warring States" to change the behavior of a young ruler who cares nothing for the misfortunes of his people. Confucius has grave doubts as to the likelihood of his success and worries that Yan will just get himself killed. He must first transform himself if he wishes to transform others.

Yan is actually a good Confucian. He knows what is right and believes it is his job is to teach it to others. He is all about yang-ing. Yang is knowing, doing, self-asserting. Zhuangzi's Confucius, on the other hand, is a thorough-going Daoist. He believes that yang can only repel yang, while yin will attract it. Yin is the emptiness that occasions the movement of yang in its direction.

Non-being the change is being the change in a yin-ish kind of way. It is what helps others to change while leaving them to think "they did it themselves". (*Laozi* 17) Did they? They did and they did not.

II

Do we need to justify our caring about the state of human affairs and our wanting to improve things? When we express skepticism about the universal applicability of our ethical norms or go still further and declare all ethical questions moot from the perspective Dao, we are told that we must then justify our caring. But this is rationalism speaking. Zhuangzi uses reason to overturn the belief that reason can show us how best to live; why then should he be required to provide reasoned justifications for his proposed alternative?

That alternative is simply to live out our humanity as it manifests. We care. What other justification is required? In the final analysis, this is the only foundation upon which we live, whether we cling to rationalism or not. This is the point of Zhuangzi's critique of reason—its validity rests entirely in human belief. For this reason we do well to make use of it, but not to the point of letting it trump the unmediated expression of our humanity.

This is what spontaneity is all about. It is living our lives in immediacy. It is trusting ourselves. And this is nothing other than entrusting ourselves to the Totality. The affirmation of the self-expression is the affirmation of all things; there cannot be the one without the other. Saying yes to our human experience is saying yes to everything.

The Daoist strategy for change-making arises from our self-experience and our understanding of how the world manifests. We and the world are a happening without an apparent Cause. We are a becoming that lacks any claim to being. It is the emptiness at our core that moves us. It is our emptiness that moves others. "Dao does nothing, but nothing is left undone." (*Laozi* 37)

This is non-being the change.

III

The fifth of the Inner Chapters is full of examples of fictional sages non-being the change. The fact that they are all misfits in some sense or another helps to highlight the fact that there are forces at work that go beyond typical yang-ist human values. They are not rock stars. They are not charismatic gurus. For the most part they simply go about their own business, and that suffices to change others.

One of these sages has lost a foot as punishment for some unspecified crime, and yet people "go to him empty and return filled". If he can be said to have a method, it is "wordless instruction". Words are the embodiment of yang. Yin is the emptiness that fills others. (5:1-11)

"Hunchback Limpleg the lipless cripple" so impressed a duke that he thought physical normality an impediment. "Thus, when Virtuosity [*de*] excels, the physical form is forgotten. But people are unable to forget the forgettable, and instead forget the unforgettable—true forgetfulness!" (5:20)

What is the unforgettable most always forgotten? It is the other side of the coin that we always leave out. It is not what is said, but what wasn't said because it can't be said. It is the ever-receding horizon of our understanding. To remember it is to remember that we always forget it. And that gives us a transforming inkling of our own emptiness which, paradoxically, enables our fullness.

Philosophical Daoism turns conventional values on their head. We typically value physical beauty, success, fame. Yet Dao, like water, seeks the lowest places, those despised by the world, even while transforming all things. It's not that the lowly and deformed are superior to the honored, but that in honoring them we are helped to remember the other side of the coin.

Still, it seems that Zhuangzi is telling us that our own physical afflictions can be our best friends; for it is by them that we can soar. These physical misfits are the lucky ones. We cannot take flight in a vacuum; flight requires resistance. "Every enslavement is also an ennobling." (2:41) Or at least it can be.

IV

Socrates understood something of the value of non-being the change. When the Delphic Oracle declared him the world's wisest person, he set out to find out how this could be given his understanding that he knew nothing for sure. This, it turns out, was the heart of his wisdom. This echoes "Confucius'" instruction of Yan in the previously mentioned "fasting of the heart" passage: "You have learned the wisdom of being wise, but not the wisdom of being free of wisdom." (4:10)

Socrates thus made it his mission to find someone who was wiser than he, someone who knew things for sure. It was an ironic mission, needless to say. It soon became clear that no one knew what they were talking about. One young man on his way to court to accuse his father of murder for the killing of a slave is sure what justice is— until he meets Socrates. But Socrates does not tell him he does not know; he simply asks questions until the young man realizes for himself that he does not know. This is the Socratic Method— midwifery.

The maieutic method (intellectual midwifery) does not deliver the conclusion; it does not declare the truth; it facilitates the self-realization of truth. Like Zhuangzi's unique spin on *qi* (*ch'i*), it is "an emptiness awaiting the presence [arising] of beings". (4:9) It creates the occasion for a self-aware understanding of one's true situation.

True truth is subjective in that it is self-realized and self-aware. Self-awareness, from the Zhuangzian point of view, is inseparable from an awareness of one's suspension in utter ambiguity—one's essential emptiness. Self-realization is not the discovery of one's "true self", but rather of one's no-fixed-self.

USING THE LIGHT
I – IV

I

Zhuangzi uses the term *yiming* ("using the light") three times in the Second Chapter in a clearly technical sense; it describes his present method and its justification. Ziporyn controversially translates "the Illumination of the Obvious" and provides an extensive justification for doing so. (pp 217-8) Others have suggested "the light of Reason" or "intuitive insight". The former is compatible with Ziporyn's take, with some qualifications. The latter is not, and makes for an important distinction in the parting of ways.

Those who translate "intuitive insight" have something like the clarity of understanding realized in "enlightenment" in mind. Ziporyn correctly suggests I think that this is incompatible with Zhuangzi's overall philosophy which never overturns the essential ambiguity of our experience. Indeed, this insurmountable ambiguity is precisely what "using the light" demonstrates. Anything else is "taking one's mind as one's teacher".

Yiming does imply making use of reason. The Second Chapter is Zhuangzi's reasoned argument for the limitations of reason. He does not disparage the use of reason, but warns against its misuse. If we think that only reason can teach us how best to live, then we will sever ourselves from the more immediate and organic aspect of our human experience. "Let your mind spring to life from its rootedness in the unthinking parts of yourself." (23; p 99) This lies at the very heart of the Daoist vision: Allow and affirm the full expression of your humanity in spontaneity.

"Hence, when the understanding consciousness comes to rest in what it does not know, it has reached the utmost." (2:36) Reason is a wonderful tool, but like everything else it has its limits. Finding those limits by "using the light" of reason itself is both the fulfillment of reason and the opportunity to experience an existential immediacy that reason cannot provide.

II

Yiming ("making use of the light") can indicate using the light of reason to illuminate things or the things that are thereby illuminated. This latter is what inspires Ziporyn's rendering: The Illumination of the Obvious. Let your actual experience show you how best to live.

Some of Zhuangzi's arguments can be hard to follow; some of his mystical leaps can seem otherworldly. But in point of fact he never suggests anything other than what common sense implies. This is the whole point of his dictum: "add nothing to the process of life".

Nothing he says requires belief, where this means something has to be true. That would be to *depend on* something, and that renders one's life contingent and mediated. Rather, he suggests we entrust ourselves to "the everyday function" of life. Suspended in innate ambiguity, this immediacy requires no justification. It is this shift away from the mediation of having to know why to the immediacy of living that is the heart of Daoist practice.

Know thyself. This is the Obvious. Illuminate the self-experience. Illuminate the self-context, the "world". Live in alignment with things as they manifest, not as you would have them to be. This is Zhuangzi's philosophy in a nutshell.

III

Following Ziporyn's interpretive rendering of *yiming* as "the Illumination of the Obvious" we can ask what then is the obvious, and what can it teach us?

All three of Zhuangzi's uses of *yiming* concern his extended argument for the relative and perspectival character of our opinions and the possibility of thereby imaginatively unifying them. (2:15, 18, 29) What is obvious is that there is no fixed determinate of value. There is no discernable Idea of the Good written in Heaven. If we take Dao to mean an unambiguous "Way of Heaven", then this is not Dao as Zhuangzi imagines it. Dao, for Zhuangzi, is the unifying and equalizing in indeterminacy of all ideas of fact and value.

This implies the self-effacement of this view as well. I say that Zhuangzi "imagines" Dao thus because it is itself a chosen perspective which must ultimately dissolve into indeterminacy. It is not the "true" Dao, but just another dao. This is the best we can do, and we have no choice but to do something—we can choose our dao, but we cannot choose to have no dao. We can choose our "operating system", our world-view, but we cannot function without one.

Why choose this one? Because it obviously aligns with our experience. And this alignment, in Zhuangzi's view, makes for the most authentic and happiest way to live. Given our obvious circumstances, these are his ultimate values. They require no more justification then does existence itself.

This dao is not for everyone. It is remedial, and thus only for those who find themselves afflicted by a specific sickness, the one the

366

illumination of the obvious itself creates—an uncompromising awareness of our suspension in ambiguity, the experience of our existential dangle. There are doubtless other remedial strategies.

IV

The most important thing that the light of reason demonstrates is its own limitations, and this reveals that the entirety of the human experience is suspended in ambiguity. I call this our existential dangle.

"Hence, the Radiance of Drift and Doubt is the sage's only map. He makes no definition of what is right but instead entrusts it to the everyday function of each thing. This is what I call the Illumination of the Obvious." (2:29)

The illumination of this ambiguity creates its own illuminating radiance. We can make use of it. We can chart our course by it. It can become the defining trajectory of our dao. This again is the usefulness of the useless.

Like Buddhism, Zhuangzi's philosophy critiques the human condition and discovers its essential emptiness. Yet, whereas Buddhism largely takes this as a negation of "existence", all of which is suffering, Zhuangzi takes it as an opportunity for the affirmation of all things. This is "letting them all bask in the broad daylight of Heaven. And that too is only a case of going by the rightness of the present 'this'." (2:16) All is well. All things are affirmable just as they manifest.

Consider and affirm New York City as you would a hill of ants. Do you see how this point of view can break us out of the cocoon of our anthropocentric preoccupation with right and wrong, affirmable and unaffirmable? Once released, we do not abandon our concern for the self-flourishing of humanity; only now its incredible dysfunction need not overwhelm us. After a good laugh, we can get busy helping our fellow-ants.

WRITING PRACTICE
I – III

I

Kierkegaard wrote that philosophers construct magnificent intellectual castles and then live in broken-down shanties beside them. For all his tortured attempts to do otherwise, we must assume that he did likewise if only in that he failed to fully realize his own vision however down-to-earth it might have been.

I take this as the norm. I do not believe. Whether there are now or have ever been fully realized sages remains moot—I have no basis for believing so. Such a belief would only serve to draw me out and away from the only reality I know—my own. And I am certainly no sage for all my blabber about sagacity.

This need not negate the value of philosophizing or the practice of writing that it typically inspires. For it is in fact a practice. It is a method by which one hopes to approximate something of what one imagines. If this seems less than ideal, so much the better. The real is all that matters.

Thus, the value of this practice requires self-honesty. And this in turn requires making publicly clear the disconnect between words and reality. My disconnect. It is done.

II

If writing can be *a* practice it is only because it *is* practice. A point of view is largely a mental construct, and in thinking things through by way of writing one incrementally tweaks it. One practices a new way of thinking. Yet, there must obviously be other still more powerful determining forces involved. Otherwise, the desired paradigm shift would be easily accomplished; and we know that it is not.

One of these forces, the egoic-self that thinks it really exists in some concrete way, is largely a habit. If it is indeed possible to experience that one "has not yet begun to exist" as Zhuangzi has Yan do, then the habitual nature of the self is established. We needn't take his word for it, however. Our core emptiness is an obvious and ever-present experience.

Is the egoic-self a "bad" habit? We must assume that it has had an important and positive role to play in the evolutionary process. We *have* survived after all. However messy in psychological and sociological terms it might be, it has helped us through the messiness of evolutionary existence. The valuation of self is thus a question of utility; it is not a moral issue, or one that pertains to the health and happiness of the cosmos.

This being the case, we can also ask if we are not ready to move beyond this habit to something more psychologically, sociologically and environmentally friendly. Daoism suggests we are. The egoic-self has served its purpose, but its beneficial contributions have mostly long expired. Might it not be time to move on? Might not our continued survival require it?

I have now written about this possibility. Has anything changed? Certainly not discernably so. Yet still it seems to be a necessary first step. And evolution takes time.

III

If this is my practice, then you the reader are only a secondary consideration. Hopefully, this is reassuring. No one likes to be preached at. It helps to know that the preacher is really just preaching to himself. Nothing said here is not addressing some perceived lack in myself.

Not that we don't share the same fundamental lacks. One value of a shared self-exploration is that we can learn through the processing of another without that directly telling us what to think or how to behave. That would be the antithesis of the approach of philosophical Daoism.

This latter is of only tertiary importance in any case. The primary benefit is the implied suggestion that one also engage in self-inquiry. What one subsequently uncovers is likely to be similar, but may lead to different responses altogether.

This begins and ends in freedom from all things fixed. None of it is required. Nothing is prescribed. It's all optional. It *is* all about freedom, after all.

Know thyself also means think for yourself; and the former can only be accomplished by way of the latter.

THE PROBLEM OF GOOD
I – VII

I

Embrace the good
And the bad shall rule.
Cling to hope
And despair will cling to you.
—Chen Jen

(Chen Jen is one of my made-up sages. I find that I agree with them most, while not taking them too seriously.)

Traditionally, philosophy and theology concern themselves with "the problem of evil". This is especially the case with the latter, where the goodness of an omnipotent God needs to be reconciled with its co-existence with evil.

Philosophical Daoism, needless to say, turns this on its head. The problem of evil is just as much the problem of good. And since the default mentality that poses the problem as concerning evil fails to see this, Daoism finds value in taking the contrary tack. Such a gadfly philosophy it is.

Without good, there would be no evil, and vice versa. Embracing the one creates the other. But why would we want to embrace the good? Because we dislike evil. What then is the motivating factor that determines our choice? Evil. In this way, evil rules; evil decides our actions.

So as to alleviate unnecessary aggravation, let's cut to the chase and say that Daoism is all in for the good. Only it is a good that has no relationship whatsoever with evil. It is what naturally arises, not as an intellectualized and mediated moral construct, but as an expression of our humanity. This is the goodness of the sage: "To do this without knowing it, and not because you have defined it as right, is called Dao." (2:23; with modifications)

II

Zhuangzi's treatment of the opposites "this" and "that" covers a wide range of issues. Primarily, he wishes to show the relative character of our opinions as determined by our unavoidably situated points of view. In this case the terms stand for subject and object, self and other. However, the word for "this" also means "right" and "that" also means "wrong". My opinion is right while the other's is wrong. Thus, the same arguments that apply to self and other—that they are mutually generating opposites—also apply to right and wrong.

"This" generates "that", and vice versa. Thus, every "this" is also a "that" and every "that" is also a "this; every self is also an object to another self, and every right is also another's wrong. "So is there really any 'this' versus 'that', any right versus wrong?" (2:17)

This being the case, Zhuangzi suggests we unite them all to form a oneness. This takes us out and beyond our "normal human inclinations". This is his psychological Dao. "When 'this' and 'that'—right and wrong—are no longer coupled as opposites—that is called the Dao as Axis, the axis of all daos." (2:17)

This does not lead the sage to lawlessness. To the contrary, the sage now "goes by the 'rightness' of the present 'this'". (2:23) Everything has become good and acceptable. Good has not been abandoned, but rather finds a new expression de-coupled from its opposite. It now arises from Dao. Dao is the affirmation of all things because all things are Dao.

It also arises from our common humanity as an expression of a new desire for universal flourishing. In the union of self and other self-flourishing becomes universal-flourishing.

As genuine human concerns right and wrong still remain coupled as opposites. The sage concerns herself with them as would anyone else, only now she also makes use of a broader perspective, one that frees her from an unexamined anthropocentrism. She walks two roads at once.

III

Is there right and wrong on Mars? Was there good and evil in the Jurassic? It seems that when we absent humanity good and evil disappear. So, this must be uniquely our problem. And it *is* a problem. And we need to deal with it as such.

But the cosmos is bigger than our new and tiny world and its concerns. Do we want to understand ourselves in a broader context? Isn't this what has been happening since the Enlightenment? We are no longer the center of everything. Everything is no longer about us. The "meaning of life" has lost its answer.

Philosophical Daoism is a response to this enlightened point of view. It is inspired by the "Illumination of the Obvious". It suggests we move beyond the hocus-pocus of religious belief (which can manifest in many apparently non-religious ways) and understand and creatively respond to the actual facts of our circumstance.

Part of this response is to put our concerns about right and wrong in context. Relativizing our concerns frees us from bondage to them. We have them still, only now they are not such a heavy burden. Indeed, now we could make the burden itself an occasion "to chariot upon what is true to both Heaven and earth, riding upon the back-and-forth of the six atmospheric breathes, so that your wandering could nowhere be brought to a halt. You would then be depending on—what?" (1:8)

You would depend on no particular outcome, whether good or evil, but would be unburdened even as you took upon yourself the heaviest of burdens.

IV

What is the good? That which brings universal flourishing. Why? Because everything wants to flourish. The good is agreement with existence; no other foundation is possible. What does it mean to flourish? To experience the fullest possible expression of one's potential. For this reason, we do well to attempt the good.

Longevity is a good. We do well to attempt to live out our "allotted years". But we might get cut off before our time just the same. From the perspective of Daoism, this is also good. Long life or short, the sage considers this of no great ultimate importance. "No one lives longer than a dead child." (2:32)

There is thus a good that transcends our everyday determinations of good and bad. This is "the rightness of the present 'this'". This is the affirmation of all happenings within the Great Happening because they are that Happening. There is no ultimate rift in the fabric of Reality. This is how we imagine it for the sake of our own flourishing.

We also see that "the trails of right and wrong are hopelessly tangled and confused." (2:39) What's right for one may be wrong for another. What's more, what's right for the one may result in bad for the other. The snake's good is the frog's bad. Life requires the death of others. We eat to survive; and although, like the Jains, we may go to extremes to avoid this, still our very existence requires the ceaseless death of others, both living and inanimate. Our very bodies are in constant warfare, and their continuation requires the death of countless others.

When we "break the jade" to make a sacred vessel we kill it. Even things seek their own flourishing in the perpetuity of their identity.

Thus, we can say that "universal flourishing" is the good, but must remember that it remains forever compromised and fraught with ambiguity. Existence is a messy business. The Daoist adopts the perspective that sees that all is well (good) despite its all being a Great Mess from top to bottom. This facilitates her self-flourishing.

V

If we take universal flourishing as our ideal understanding of the everyday good, then we have a guiding principle by which to live well in the world. However, since our decisions and actions in this regard are most always necessarily compromised in that the flourishing of one thing usually requires the non-flourishing of another, we must admit to our dwelling in perpetual ambiguity.

Some Daoist and Confucian thought imagines a sage so insightful as to be capable of sorting out her decisions in perfect harmony with every situation in its total context. Zhuangzi, I think, might again quote an ancient proverb and call this "fleeing the Lord's dangle". His response to life pivots on the unavoidable ambiguity that permeates our every experience. This is the obvious. The other is religious idealism.

Thus, we remain essentially at sea despite our having a moral compass. Fortunately, we also have sails by which to steer by that compass, though we do not know where we are eventually going or what hazards might lay on our chosen course.

It is also fortunate that it will all work out well in the end. Unless, of course, we take the cosmos as evil; for if any evil endures, no Totality is imaginable.

VI

How do we arrive at universal flourishing as our everyday good? It is rooted in the imaginative equalization of all things. This is the central theme of Zhuangzi's second chapter. The title of this chapter (*Qiwulun*) can be taken as speaking to the equalization of our *theories* about things or of the things themselves. Since our world is a cognitive creation, these amount to the same thing.

Ziqi has lost his "me". He explains this experience through the very dense metaphor of the response of the forest trees to the wind (*qi*) belched forth by the Great Clump. (2:1ff) Each tree makes its own unique sound, though they are all the same in responding to the one wind. Yet no "doer" can be found. Neither the wind nor the trees can be said to be the *cause* of these expressions. They spontaneously arise.

So too is it for Ziqi who cannot find any actual "doer" in himself—he has lost his "me". Like Yan, he has experientially understood that he "has not yet begun to exist". (4:10) He is a spontaneously arising happening, not a concrete fixed self.

This experience of the (provisional) loss of one's "counterpart", the objective side of the I-me self-experience, is also the loss of the objectified world, the world as something different than oneself. More simply, Ziqi has realized a sense of oneness with all things.

"Heaven and earth were born together with me, and the ten thousand things and I are one," exclaims Zhuangzi. (2:32)

This equalization of the cognitive construct of self and other transfers self-concern to world-concern. We care for the flourishing of all things because we are all things, and caring for what we are is inseparable from being at all. Our self-caring becomes our world-caring.

Nothing is quite so simple, however. In the real world, compromise is necessary. There are natural conflicts between the needs of things, and our self-caring must frequently trump our world-caring. For though we may have lost our "me", our "I" remains just the same. The primary, organic self-caring that energizes our world-caring is our first responsibly.

Our awareness of the oneness of things still obtains, nevertheless. Where all things are one, nothing can be lost. This is "hiding the world in the world".

VII

In its imaginative equalization of all things and the consequent cosmo-centric recontextualization of an otherwise individual- and species-centric world-view philosophical Daoism translates into universal caring.

All things have their right to be. All things exist for themselves. Nothing exists solely for the use of humanity or any single individual. Nothing is to be completely objectified. All things are treasured.

Paralleling Zhuangzi's pronouncement on the mutual goodness of life and death we can say: If my existence is good, so also is the existence of all other things. In having psychologically identified with the Totality our self-love transfers to a love for all things.

This is philosophical Daoism's organic foundation for environmental justice. Tree- and boulder-hugging are as natural as hugging one's child. And if there is pleasure in the latter, how much more pleasure awaits the opening of our hearts to all things?

WORDS
I – X

I

Words are by their nature a great yanging. They assert. They declare. They impose.

Zhuangzi suggests there is also a "wordless instruction" (5:2), a teaching by way of example. And in this instance, that example is stillness, wordlessness, itself: "People cannot see their reflections in running water, but only in still water. Only stillness can still the multitude to the point of genuine stillness." (5:9)

How do we know this? Words.

Even were we to assume that Zhuangzi realized what he preached (which I do not), how could he teach anyone but his few disciples (if he had any) except through words?

Zhuangzi thus sought to convey his teaching through words that were also imbued with yin. This is the hallmark of his writing as noted by several of his interpreters. "Vague! Ambiguous!" (33; p 124) We might add: Fantastic! Unbelievable! Ridiculous! Untruthful! Contradictory!

But that would not be original: "He used ridiculous and far-flung descriptions, absurd and preposterous sayings, senseless and shapeless phrases, indulging himself unrestrainedly as the moment demanded, uncommitted to any one position, never looking at things exclusively from any one corner." (33; p 123) Whew! And to think that we sometimes take him literally.

This all makes perfect sense, of course, given his commitment to not-knowing as an invitation to a transcendent leap into "far-flung and unfettered wandering" "in our homeland of not even anything".

II

Zhuangzi used a lot of words to talk about the unreliability of words. They represent things, but they can never be those things; nor can they ever truly reach the fullness of their meaning since they must necessarily draw a limiting circle around them. The "meaning" of things is their complete context, and that is boundless. They are all mystery.

It is also the case that, when speaking of that boundless context—Chaos, Dao, Mystery—words are their own contradiction. We see this in his discussion of the One. There is One, he suggests. But then he adds that One plus the word makes two, and mention of that makes three. Words are the consequence of not-oneness and are its expression. Like most everything else, they are great—they just need to know their limitations.

Thus, Zhuangzi used various strategies to put his words in their proper place. And in doing so, he was able to convey his message as his medium—a kind of "wordless teaching" full of words.

In one instance, he has his (obviously fictitious sage—itself a strategy) get specific about the character of a sage, but only after that sage admits that these are "reckless words". (2:41) This is not only an admission of their inadequacy, but also of their danger. His disciple might be so foolish as to take them literally. Thus, he also says that these words must be listened to "recklessly"—that is, in full awareness of their hypothetical and hyperbolic nature.

The hearer has her or his responsibility to season things with a proper dose of yin.

Various of his early interpreters recognized Zhuangzi's distinctive style and identified some of these strategies. These will be discussed in the following posts.

III

The author of the final chapter of the *Zhuangzi* suggests that Zhuangzi used three types of words to communicate his message with those he thought "incapable of conversing seriously with himself". (33; p 123) My sense is that he did not understand Zhuangzi's motivation at all, and that this was a consequence of his not really grasping his message. Still, there's lots to learn from his analysis.

The author of the 27th chapter, "Words Lodged Elsewhere", provides a very similar description of his *own* words, some of which are in verbatim agreement with those of the 33rd chapter just mentioned. (p 114) Perhaps both authors discussed Zhuangzi's philosophy at the Jixia Academy which flourished in the late Fourth Century BCE.

It seems that the author of the 27th chapter was representing himself as Zhuangzi, but scholarship would likely demonstrate that this is not from the hand of Zhuangzi. He was in effect making use of Zhuangzi's own methodological deception.

The most interesting description of Zhuangzi's words calls them "spill-over goblet words". This was a special vessel used for ritual purposes. It was hinged in such a way that it tipped and emptied when full. By analogy, Zhuangzi's words are able to give "unbroken extension of his meanings" and to "give forth new meanings without shedding the old ones."

Statements are typically fixed in the presentation of their meaning. Over time those meanings either become obsolete or continue to hold their own. Not so those of Zhuangzi, suggest these authors. Their very ambiguity allows new meanings to be discovered in them without contradicting previous meanings.

This is a sophisticated approach to truth and evinces a genuine appreciation of Zhuangzi's eschewal of fixed truth. Whether these authors were able to follow this through to the logical end—that there is really no knowable truth at all—is another matter. The author of the 33rd chapter clearly was not as evinced in his belief in "*the* [perfect] ancient art of the Dao".

IV

"Spill-over goblet words" are words that self-empty once their meaning has been understood. This puts us in mind of words attributed to Zhuangzi in which he suggests we forget words once we have understood their meaning: "Words are for the intent. When you have got hold of the intent, you forget the words. Where can I find a man who has forgotten words, so I can have a few words with him?" (26; p 114)

How can it be that words and their meaning are two different things? How can we forget the one and retain the other?

Most fundamentally, words can only *represent* things—they are not the things themselves. The meaning is the thing itself. If someone says, "This is a tree", this tells us a lot; we are now able to apply yet more descriptive words to it. We "understand" it better; but we have yet to experience it.

Can we experience a tree?

If we can, this would mean that a vast world of experience is available to us. Not only trees, but every other thing could be experienced beyond their superficial representation in words.

Isn't "awe" descriptive of an experience of something beyond words? We can be "in awe" in the presence of a majestic redwood. We are affected by it in some visceral way.

What if we could experience everything in this way? What if a dust mite could leave us in awe? Or the dust particle it calls home? How are they the same as the majestic redwood? They are an incredible mystery.

The mystery of things is not simply their unknowableness; it is also that they are simply "there". And this "meaning" is an experience beyond words. Mystery is an experience. A pleasurable one.

V

Zhuangzi's use of Confucius is especially instructive. No matter how serious the message put in his mouth, there is a humorous side to it. Things are not quite as fixed and sure as they might immediately seem to be. We are reminded to take it all with a grain of salt.

The author of the 33rd chapter seems to have missed this: Zhuangzi provides "citations of weighty authorities for verification, words put in the mouth of others for broad acceptance." (p 123) Again, he seems to have missed the indispensable irony. But then for him there *is* a True Dao (Path) that needs expressing (albeit it now, lamentably expressed in only fragmented parts). It's all very serious.

Sometimes Zhuangzi's Confucius is the consummate spokesperson for Zhuangzi's "Daoism". Sometimes, he is the polar opposite of that view. Sometimes he gets that he doesn't get it and begs to be the disciple of his own disciple who does get it; other times he realizes his own dao will just have to do. (Daos are unavoidable though the one chosen is a matter of personal preference *and* ability.)

This is Zhuangzi at play. We are invited to play along.

VI

"But human speech is not just the blowing of air. Speech has something *of which* it speaks, something it refers to. Yes, but what it refers to is peculiarly unfixed... You take it to be different from the chirping of baby birds. But is there really any difference between them?" (2:14)

To my thinking, this equation of human speech to the chirping of baby birds invites one of Zhuangzi's most powerful imaginative exercises. Just going there for a moment can be truly mind-expanding. Being shaken out of our self-absorbed anthropocentrism can be an exhilarating experience.

What may seem at first like a negation can in fact be profoundly affirming. There is unity in Nature, and we are invited to experientially return to our participation in it. Ultimately, this entails the exchange of a fixed-identity for identification with "The Great Openness". It's a pretty good deal all in all.

Pascal's Wager has relevance here: "He is no fool who gives up what he cannot keep to gain what he cannot lose." Nothing beyond a temporal enhancement of the quality of life is "gained", of course. (Pascal had salvation in mind.) All is as it is, in any event. No need to mend a cosmic rift is imagined.

There is, of course, also that sense in which human speech *is* different from the chirping of baby birds. It's just that words cannot carry the weight of truth which we wish to place upon them. They are "peculiarly unfixed". Their foundation is ultimately vacuous.

So let's have fun with words. Let's play the hand we've been dealt as best we can, while not taking things so seriously as to destroy all the fun.

VII

Huizi's chief criticism of Zhuangzi's philosophy was that his words were "big but useless". (1:15) For the rationalist, the utility of words stops at their ability to designate a fixed and sure meaning.

The "rectification of names" was a central concern for philosophers of many stripes in Zhuangzi's time. If we could just make absolutely clear and fixed what words mean, then we would have a Dao that could be spoken. Then we would have sure, cognitive guidance. We could take our minds as our teacher.

Confucius purportedly (this may be a later interpolation) declared the rectification of names the "first thing to be done" if we want to transform society: "If names be not correct, language is not in accordance with the truth of things. If language be not in accordance with the truth of things, affairs cannot be carried on to success." (*Analects* 13; Legge)

The Daoist revolution, as seen in the opening statement of the *Laozi*, emphatically declared that no such cognitively fixed guidance was possible: "The dao that can be spoken is not the genuine Dao."

So, if we are to forget Zhuangzi's words once we have grasped their meaning, what is that meaning? Only more words can say it, but it cannot be spoken. A bit of a conundrum, it seems. But this need not stop us: "Where is the man who has forgotten words that I might have a few words with him?"

Here are a few words about his meaning: There is the possibility of wandering in freedom if we depend on no words—though we must make use of them to imagine it.

This is a possible psychological response to our experience in life. Words would have us make it *the correct* response. But forgetting words disallows our doing so. This can be the crux of it. There is a cutting off of fixity, since it is words that are inherently fixed.

Being unfixed is the capacity to wander.

VIII

Words written about things "spiritual", given a certain temporal remove (actual or fabricated—think The Book of Mormon), frequently become "scripture". And scripture easily becomes an occasion for bibliolatry. Ironically, given God's declared distaste for idolatry, this is most common in the revealed religions wherein God had a lot to say.

God is held hostage to his own words, some of which were admittedly spoken in the heat of a momentary state of wrath. He has also made a lot of promises (See? They're written right here.)—and God is a promise-keeper, even with his stiff-necked and rebellious chosen, though it sometimes irks him to have to do so.

Because the Book is infallible, everything in it must be taken literally. God does not lie. God is not Truth; he *obeys* It.

"In the beginning was the Word, and the Word was with God, and the Word was God." (1John 1:1) There you have it. Let us then worship *Logos*—the Word—the Book.

Disrespect the Book and we will kill you—irrespective of what it might say about not killing.

Nor are the more intuitive religions free from bibliolatry. "The Buddha *said* ..." Really? Belief, it seems, requires fixed truths. (Zen tries to overcome this by advocating experience "outside the Scriptures". "If you meet the Buddha, kill him.")

Multitudes have been murdered because a mosque sat (now razed) on the supposed birth spot of an "historical" Rama, the hero of the fantastic tale of the *Ramayana*, now taken quite literally.

This bit of sarcasm is intended as a reminder of our near universal tendency to turn words into Truth. The consequence is more often than not closed- and bloody-mindedness.

I would suggest that Zhuangzi's words have no more Truth in them than these present ramblings. They are just the scribblings of another work in progress—a work that has no end—a work that is its own end, even if unendingly open-ended.

As always, there's freedom to be had somewhere in understanding this apparent mess.

IX

Our visceral responses to words are quite instructive. "Sticks and stones can break my bones, but words can never hurt me" is a familiar childhood chant. They often *do* hurt, of course, which is why we have concocted this counter-spell.

This returns us to Song Xing's "To be insulted is not a disgrace" (1:7; 33; p 121)—his own counter-spell. If we can achieve an unflappable self-esteem, words cannot hurt us. Zhuangzi, as we have seen, suggests we not even depend on that, but rather abandon our sense of a fixed and vulnerable self altogether.

Words are thus quite useful even—especially—in their potentially negative impacts. An insult is something upon which to soar, or to at least make the attempt. It's all good training.

The propensity for an exchange of words to devolve into conflict is another fine teaching moment. "They begin nicely enough, but in the end it gets ugly... Words are like wind and waves..." (4:15) As every sailor knows, wind means waves, and it's the waves that are the scary and harmful bit. Similarly, there is nothing like the onset of an argument to demonstrate our continued dependence on self-esteem and belief in the truth of our opinions.

We can be thankful, therefore, for the downside of words as well as the upside. If we want a teacher, there is nothing better than our own everyday silliness.

X

"Skillful barking does not make a dog good, and skillful talking does not make a man even a worthy, much less a great man." (24; p 105)

Taken somewhat out of its context this observation provides an opportunity to make yet another disclaimer. Sometimes after writing a post I feel genuine pleasure in having skillfully barked. Or at least so it seems to me.

Perhaps there are moments when this makes me feel like a good dog, but for the most part I suffer little from that particular delusion. For whatever personal reason I may wish the reader to know that, it is in point of fact important that she or he do so. It is doubtful that any would take me as "a worthy, much less a great man"; rather, the true point is that *no one* is, or at least that we must be very cautious— "like crossing a river in winter"—when admiring the barking of any dog, no matter how skillful.

The context of this sentence quoted above is a speech given by "Confucius" at a feast given in his honor. At his most "Daoist", he proceeds to extol the virtue of "wordless words". An example of this, he declares, can be seen in the example of one of the attendees. As his army was arrayed before another on the verge of battle, he fell asleep with "a feathered fan" in his hand. Seeing such apparent confidence (actually insouciance), the opposing army stood down. This was indeed a "wordless word"—a "good word".

Confucius goes on to extol the virtues of a truly "Great Man": "Nothing is more complete than heaven and earth, but do they become so by seeking to be so? One who understands the great completeness seeks nothing, loses nothing, abandons nothing, never letting mere beings alter who he is. He returns only to his own self, yet he finds it inexhaustible. He follows the ancients, but never becomes their mere copy".

This is a truly wonderful passage, one worthy of our serious and prolonged imaginative engagement. In furthering my point regarding caution, however, I will only step back and suggest that we would do well to remember that such a Great Man is only an ideal—and understanding *that* is what allows us to "return to our own self".

MISCELLANEOUS
REFLECTIONS

ON THE CONTRIBUTIONS
OF THE MAD

As I attempt to write this next book I am constantly challenged by my sense of inadequacy, just as I have been with every previous similar endeavor. I am, quite frankly, not really up to the task. I lack the scholarship, the intellectual capacity, and the will to do the very hard work that attempting to at least partially overcome these deficiencies would require. I am an amateur. Yet I continue nevertheless. For the most part, this is because this is how I teach myself. The idea that any of what I write will be of genuine use to you the reader is secondary, if for no other reason than that even the best of writing would probably fail of that goal in any case. Perhaps I've set the bar too high, but I really don't see much point in writing, except as pertains to one's own edification (and ego-enhancement, I suppose) if it makes no real difference in the world.

Still, I believe I have something to contribute. Though I lack the courage to even peruse my own copy of *ALL IS WELL IN THE GREAT MESS*, I believe there are significant insights within it that might at least suggest new lines of inquiry among scholars and inspire my peers to pursue their own philosophy of life along similar, though necessarily divergent, lines.

I find encouragement in the madman Jieyu's contributions to classical Chinese philosophy. He is twice mentioned in the Inner Chapters, first as one who relates a fantastic vision of a sage, and again as singing a derisive song to Confucius. In the first, his credulity becomes an occasion for a critique of its twin sister, incredulity—belief and disbelief being of the same genus and their transcendence being a matter of the spirit.

The second is a parody of the story as it appears in the *Analects* (18:5) and criticizes Confucius for his political ambitions and the inflexibility of his path. We might profitably ask why his ridicule was included in the *Analects*, a book devoted to the exaltation of Confucius. We are told that it has to do with Confucius' virtue of timeliness (which Zhuangzi disputes) and as means to answering the criticisms of an emerging Daoist challenge. But whatever the specific reasons we find Jieyu there or in the *Zhuangzi* I would suggest that it is because even in his madness he had a contribution to make.

In a world where nothing can ever be fully and comprehensively understood, even the stammerings of an amateur might have something helpful to say.

THAT SCARY THING
CALLED MYSTICISM

I cannot think of a single article or book that mentions mysticism in Daoism generally or Zhuangzi specifically that considers the possibility of a species of mysticism that lies outside one particular traditional definition. This definition holds that mysticism entails an intuitive insight into the Ultimate with which one is thereby in some way united, usually through a realization that that union has always already obtained. This, in my view, is an essentially *religious* definition since it presumes some form of positive understanding of reality. In the case of Daoism, a category into which Zhuangzi is always lumped, this means one realizes "the Dao". Is there really no other possible form of mysticism?

I call mysticism "scary" for two reasons. It is scary to me. I am not interested in doing religion. I do not want to do it. I *cannot* consciously do it (though I likely frequently fall into it by default). Those that can, are affirmed in their pursuits.

It is scary to scholars; one must be careful not to taint one's scholarship with a betrayal of actual subjective experience. Advocacy for anything other than "facts" is anathema. It is, however, acceptable to assign religious mysticism to Zhuangzi as a matter of fact. How one can speak of the subjective experience of others without any experience of that experience oneself remains a mystery to me.

There are exceptions. Among these is Chad Hansen who argues for Zhuangzi as a skeptical philosopher who doubted our ability to know anything of the Ultimate, intuitively or otherwise. I agree. But he also therefore rejects *any* mysticism in Zhuangzi, since his definition of mysticism remains within the traditional box. Ziporyn, to my thinking, does appreciate the mysticism in Zhuangzi as an expression of and response to his not-knowing, though he is careful not to advocate. His treatment of *yiming* ("making use of the light"), as "the Illumination of the Obvious" (our obvious not-knowing), instead of its typical association with "spiritual insight" (*prajna*) is indicative of this.

So, what other form of mysticism might Zhuangzi have suggested? A mysticism utterly innocent of all religious presumption of knowing anything about the Ultimate. One surrenders into utter Mystery as an act of trust. And though one is changed thereby, one emerges as clueless as ever. All is and must necessarily remain Mystery. What is Mystery? Everything is Mystery. Release into the most intimate of all possible experiences, the mysterious experience of you. Or take a walk in the woods.

Surrender, release, acceptance—these are one, and they cannot help but issue into deep trust, affirmation and thankfulness. Amen. (Oops!)

SCIENCE AND THE
RELIGIOUS MIND

This is a "review" of a book I have not read. It is more a visceral response to the genera than a comment on this particular manifestation. The book is Livia Kohn's latest, *Science and the Dao*. Here is a quote from the release blurb from Three Pines Press: "*Science and the Dao* presents a comprehensive examination of core Daoist facets from the point of view of modern science. Exploring its cosmology, physiology, psychology, cultivation, and visions of immortality in the light of astrophysics, particle physics, paleoanthropology, behavioral kinesiology, cell biology, and more, the book enhances the credibility of traditional Daoist ideas and practices, thereby making them more accessible to modern people."

It's natural to wish to demonstrate the compatibility and overlap of one's beliefs with the findings of science; one would hope that they do in fact overlap. It is the deep and likely unexamined motivation that underlies this universal need to *prove* the validity of religious belief that interests me. "[T]he book enhances the credibility of traditional Daoist ideas and practices." This need for "credibility" is perfectly legitimate within the context of religious Daoism. Ironically, science and religion, not to mention atheism, have a great deal in common when it comes to requiring "proofs" for their claims. All *belief* in "truth", scientific or otherwise, ultimately depends on proof, imagined or "demonstrated".

The permutations of this religious dependence on proof are many. Here it uses science to give "credibility" to something so incredible as immortality. Testimony of personal transformation is a common example. Supposed miracles work. Hyper-charismatic gurus do the trick. Pronouncements about being the "oldest", "purest", "richest", "biggest", "best", "fastest growing"—all attempt to give credence to belief and subtly evince a dependence on "truth".

Zhuangzian "Daoism", on the other hand, neither seeks nor requires any proofs, for it does not depend on anything being "true". There being nothing to believe, there is nothing to prove. This is at the very heart of Zhuangzi's vision. It reveals a radically different fork in the road, and this fork is not one that "modern people" are inclined to take. The religious mind is the default coping mechanism through which human beings typically respond to their irremediable existential dangle. Belief in immortality can be most comforting. Who are we to abuse them of their chosen dao?

Is philosophical Daoism therefore "better"? It is for those who cannot believe, but not for those who can. It too is just another dao, albeit one that sees Dao not as "the Dao", a metaphysical Something, but as the imagined confluence of all daos. The point of this "review" is not to prove that philosophical Daoism is better than religious Daoism, but simply to remind the reader that they are not at this level the same, though as human coping mechanisms they most certainly are. The real question is which one most authentically represents the human experience of adriftedness and cluelessness.

TRANSFORMATIVE RECONTEXTUALIZATION

I lift this phrase "transformative recontextualization" from Brook Ziporyn's *Being and Ambiguity*. I say "lifted" because, though it may indeed apply as I will use it here, he uses it in a much broader and more complicated sense—one that I will not attempt to elucidate here. To my thinking, the phrase perfectly describes Zhuangzi's suggested method for personal transformation. Consider looking at things in a different way, and see if that doesn't change how you interface with the world. It's that simple.

Much is made of Zhuangzi's perspectival relativism. Eels like it cold and clammy; humans like it warm and cozy. Every preference or theory about how best to live (or be) derives from a perspective, and since everything (Zhuangzi seems to see things as "having" a perspective) must have a perspective we would do best to allow them the space to express it (where they don't seriously negatively impact the ability of others to do so). This is his relativism. Scholars debate the species of this relativism, whether it is strong or weak, but this largely misses the point. The point is the transformation of one's interface with oneself and the world. Zhuangzi is not so much interested in questions of epistemology as he is in realizing freedom from dogmatism. This is the point of eels versus humans analogy.

Throughout the Inner Chapters we are presented with similar suggestions that we recontextualize vis-à-vis ourselves and the world. Perhaps the broadest possible recontextualization can be found in his suggestion that we "hide the world in the world". Rather than seeing ourselves as discreet monads—something that can be lost—why not instead identify with the Totality. Where in Everything can anything be lost? This is intended to address the fear of death without recourse to belief in the perpetuation of one's present identity, one's "temporary lodging".

Viewing "life and death as a single string" is another way of addressing the fear of death. Recontextualization in this case requires taking life and death as a single unit; one does not come without the other. This is the nature of things. Unlike belief in the immortality of a soul, this perspective "adds nothing to the process of life". It is how life is experienced.

These perspectival recontextualizations, and many others, all have transformative freedom as their goal. They do not advocate for the "truth" about the world. Instead, they merely suggest what might lead to a happier and more flourishing life. To Zhuangzi's thinking, most of us live cramped and stiff lives—we have chosen to sleep where it's cold and clammy. He suggests we might want to try someplace warm and cozy. In the end, nothing can be lost in any case.

How is a change in perspective transformative? At the extreme, isn't this what so-called enlightenment is all about? Nirvana is a "turning". However, at my reading, Zhuangzi suggests a much more prosaic outcome, an approximation of what might be beyond complete realization through a kind of imaginative meditation. Why would we want to burden ourselves with yet another absolutist goal?

WAS ZHUANGZI A GREAT SAGE?

Was Zhuangzi a great sage? To my thinking, this is a question of great significance, not for the answer we might choose to give, but for the fact that we would ask it at all. Why would we believe that there have ever been any sages? Why would we *need* to believe that there have ever been any sages?

On my reading, it is just such a default assumption that there is some final remedy to the "existential dangle" of the human condition as evinced in the hypothetical sage that Zhuangzi wished to overturn. If Zhuangzi was a sage, then it was only because he eschewed the belief that sagacity was some kind of final cure-all, or that it was fully realizable at all. The Zhuangzian sage dwells in "drift and doubt" and wanders free because she has abandoned pursuit of every fixed and sure mooring. As such, sagacity itself could only be an unfixed, never-arriving, but ever-approximating experience.

Yes, but did he not make continual reference to sages? He did. One subsists on only wind and dew, flies on the backs of dragons, and never ages. Another survives world conflagration unscathed. How do these fantastic stories differ from incredibly huge fish that become vast birds, trees that talk, and shadows who converse with their own shadows? Literalism has no place in the understanding of Zhuangzi. Only the religious mind would have it otherwise.

We assume that because ancient teachers speak of sagacity they must have realized it. I, too, speak of sagacity; does that make me a sage? Laozi wrote that those who speak do not know while those who know do not speak. For this, some have mocked him—for he then went on to speak. They foolishly believed that Laozi thought he knew. Needing someone to believe in, they were disappointed that he did not. Needing "the answer", they missed his message.

Zhuangzi tells us that we would be far better off forgetting about sages and getting on with "evolving along our own daos". And evolution, as we know, is a messy affair. Like life itself.

WAS ZHUANGZI A PHILOSOPHER?

Was Zhuangzi really a philosopher? Of course he was. However, there is a sense in which he was not, and that sense, I believe, is at the heart of his philosophy.

Ultimately, Zhuangzi's philosophy vanishes into itself. It self-immolates. It is a philosophy of life that advocates for such an unmediated living of life that there remains no room or need for philosophizing.

Typically, philosophy attempts to answer questions about how best to live, think and behave. If we say, for instance, that our highest value is the collective flourishing of all things, philosophy asks after our *justifications* for such an assertion. On what basis can we make such an assertion? Upon what sound and well-reasoned foundation does our assertion rest? Following Zhuangzi we must reply, on no foundation. It happens. And what happens neither requires nor admits to logical justification. We might inquire as to how a tree grows, but we cannot discover why it grows. It grows.

Thus, when Zhuangzi suggests that we do not take our logical mind as our teacher and thereby add to the process of life, he is both doing philosophy and advocating for not-doing philosophy. It is curious how his most logical and reasoned arguments are for precisely the ultimate abandonment of the need for any such thing. But has he abandoned them? Obviously not.

His philosophy calls for the abandonment of philosophy, yet even in its abandonment it returns to philosophy. It self-immolates, but like the Phoenix it rises again from its own ashes. If "return is the movement of the Dao", then nothing is ever lost. Nor does a final Entropy reign; return is inexhaustible.

This should not surprise us; for the transformation of things is not their negation. The reasoning mind is the human mind, and this too is affirmed. Only Zhuangzi would have us consign it to the fire that it might rise again, transformed. Our philosophizing will then be a kind of not-philosophizing; our reasoning minds will romp and play within their limitations, truly integrated into the process of life.

The reader likely wearies of hearing about walking two roads at once, yet this writer finds it everywhere he turns.

ZHUANGZI WAS NOT A DAOIST

Scholars like to point out that none of the so-called Daoist masters were Daoists. I would similarly assert that neither were they "masters", but that's a topic for another post. It was not until the Western Han historian Sima Tan (c. 165–110 BCE) organized the various strains of philosophy that emerged during the Warring States era (480-222 BCE) that there came to be "schools". The *daojia* designates the School of Daoism. Zhuangzi wrote two hundred years prior to this *ex facto* classification.

I have never had any real problem with this designation, and have seen the issue as yet another occasion for scholarship to get lost in minutiae rather than actually engaging with the philosophies themselves. There is, however, a serious problem that arises from this classification when the philosophies themselves are interpreted in the context of a larger understanding of "Daoism". The philosophies lose their distinctiveness in being made to conform to what supposedly describes them all. This is glaringly the case in Livia Kohn's *Zhuangzi: Text and Context*, yet another interpretation of Zhuangzi that ignores his radical departure from other so-called Daoists in making him part of a larger imagined and fabricated whole.

One supposed solution to this problem is to understand *daojia* as a *lineage*, an evolving philosophy rather than a fixed school. This suggests that Daoism was improved over time. Fung Yu-lan (*A Taoist Classic: Chuang-Tzu*, p 117) makes this assertion. But this is again a means of dismissing the unique character of each philosophy in favor of a now fuller Daoism. This very need for a "perfected" view is itself indicative of a human inclination that Zhuangzi sought to overturn. Religious Daoism especially feels the need to "prove" itself through its lineage. Yet none of this has even a remote place in Zhuangzi's philosophy though he is nonetheless subsumed into that lineage.

Fung Yu-lan sometimes seems to discern the spirit of Zhuangzi's philosophy, especially as it pertains to the ability to walk two roads at once, but then he undermines it by making him a "Daoist" and telling us that Daoism (and therefore Zhuangzi) "opposed" all human institutions as artificial and "despised" all knowledge (p 19). This is not the position of Zhuangzi.

For this reason it seems necessary to declare that Zhuangzi was not a Daoist. His message is a radical departure from the already religiously inclined projects of his proto-Daoist contemporaries and cannot be subsumed in those that followed. He is not part of a Daoist lineage. He stands alone—not as a "great master", but as a great non-master. And that means that worrying about any of this is to have missed the point of his philosophy.

ZHUANGZI WAS A BULL-SHIT ARTIST

If the traditional paragons of virtuosity were great successes, says Zhuangzi, then so is he and everyone else. They were, and so is he and so are we. They were not, and neither is he and nor either are we. Whenever we take something as "fully formed" (*cheng*), as complete and finished, then we have left something out, and that is missing the most important thing of all. What is it? The sage holds it in her embrace and does not say, answers Zhuangzi. But let us be poor disciples and say: What is left out is success if we think anything a failure, and failure if we think anything a success. This understanding is what the sage embraces and what cannot be said. For to say it, is to "fully form" it and leave out the most important something once again.

No one has lived a fuller life than a dead infant, and the long-lived Pengzu died too young. Everything is complete and perfect. Everything is a total mess. Everything is empty. Everything is full.

Zhuangzi was a great Master. Zhuangzi was a bull-shit artist just like me.

We often hear and read of great Zen or Daoist masters, but seldom of great Zen and Daoist bull-shit artists. Why? Because we hunger for the "fully formed"; we are chronically inclined to the comfort of the religious mind. We want the great Answer, the True Way, the Sure Anchor. We want to be other than human, and if someone else has managed it, then perhaps so can we. Indeed, they have already managed it for us.

Words must choose a side; they must make a statement. When all the world chooses the "fully formed", we would do best to speak of adriftedness and doubt. When the human mind defaults to the belief that any of these bull-shit artists were great "masters", we would do best to affirm the former. Zhuangzi was no different than you or I. He had a vision of a happier way to live his existential dangle and he found some joy in attempting to realize it and in sharing it. Because he knew this, because he embraced this in his heart, he was a great master. He was a great master because he knew there is no such thing, or rather, that there is no one who is not. Or both. Or neither.

POSTSCRIPT

"Daos are made by walking them," Zhuangzi tells us. But if that's the case, then there are as many daos as there are pairs of feet to walk them, since everyone walks their own unique road.

Zhuangzi grew his own dao while engaging with the many other daos of his time. Among his many interpreters in the book that bears his name new daos evolved. Indeed, for more than two millennia a multitude of new daos have arisen in part through engagement with Zhuangzi. What I written here is just one more.

We might wish to take Zhuangzi for a sage, but he tells us to that we would be far better off forgetting all sages and "evolving along our own daos."

Surely I needn't worry about anyone taking me for a sage, but it bears repeating that all I have spun here is offered as merely an example of one possible engagement with Zhuangzi and life itself. The chief goal has been to inspire, not to instruct.

Still, it seems to me that there's *some* good stuff in all these words, and who knows, perhaps some of these might even become useful paving stones in the evolving of your own dao.

CPSIA information can be obtained
at www.ICGtesting.com
Printed in the USA
BVHW07s2124051018
529449BV00001B/2/P